INCREDIBLE
STORIES

*In loving memory of Jackie McLeod-Roberts (1942–2002).
Tenacious, compassionate, rigorous – a true scientist.*

Acknowledgements

To make the programmes in the series *Incredible Stories* we filmed in Europe, Africa, North and South America. Along the way we were helped by an enormous number of different people, from academics to local guides. As is almost always the case in programme-making, people were most helpful and generous with both their time and their expertise. We could not have made the series – nor this book – without them and I give them all my thanks. The conclusions that have been drawn from the evidence and, of course, any mistakes in the writing of this book are my own.

My greatest debt is to my colleagues on the *Incredible Stories* team at Granada Television in Manchester who ferreted out the information to tell these stories in a new way and who have shown their professionalism and talent in the entertaining, revealing and visually attractive programmes they have made.

Mark Atkinson, Phil Buckley, Sarah Cain, Paul Clarke, Peter Connors, Jenny Greep, Tim Hopewell, Alex Horsfall, Kim Horton, Tim Pollard, Ivan Probert, Karen Stockton, Dion Stuart, Ruth Swarbrick, Jo Walker, Gareth Williams, Mike Woolmans.

I hope you know how much you are appreciated.

Liz McLeod is Executive Producer of Granada Television's series *Incredible Stories* and was Editor of the *Savage* series for Granada, broadcast on itv1. She is the author of *Savage Planet* published by Granada Media and lives near Lancaster.

INCREDIBLE
STORIES

World Mysteries Explained

LIZ MCLEOD

GRANADA

First published by Granada Media, 2002
An imprint of André Deutsch Ltd
20 Mortimer Street
London
W1T 3JW

In Association with Granada Media Group

A catalogue record of this book is available from the British Library

ISBN 0 233 05073 6

Picture credits:
Big Foot: Big Hoax? – Tim Hopewell/GTV
The Curse of King Tutankhamun's Tomb – Jenny Greep/GTV;
Gareth Williams/The Tutankhamun Exhibition
The Mystery of the Nasca Lines – NASA; Aurelio Rodriguez; Paul Clarke/GTV
The Ten Plagues of Egypt – Gareth Williams/GTV; Neil Marland/GTV
The Lost City of Atlantis – Paul Clarke/GTV
The Mystery of the Bermuda Triangle – Neil Marland/GTV
In Search of the Real Vampire Hunters – Tim Hopewell/GTV

Typeset by E-Type, Liverpool

1 3 5 7 9 10 8 6 4 2

CONTENTS

CHAPTER 1

Big Foot: Big Hoax?

It's bigger than a man – far bigger. It's elusive. And hyper-intelligent.

It will eat anything and everything and it has immense strength, ripping up boulders and twisting tree branches.

Though few people have ever had a really good long look at it, sightings of the beast are reported every year, from places scattered all over northern and western North America.

The native peoples of the west coast call it Sasquatch. The tabloid newspapers know it as 'Big Foot'.

To millions, Big Foot is simply a joke. But the legend is tenacious and now a growing number of committed Sasquatch investigators are trying to introduce scientific method into the search for Big Foot.

Can all the evidence they have gathered still be dismissed as a hoax?

The evidence for Big Foot starts with stories: hunters' tales, Native Indian tales, travellers' tales. From the early nineteenth century, when European explorers first reached the west coast of America, stories of a huge creature living in the remote mountains and forests of the area have circulated, in books and stories, in newspapers and magazines. Since the early twentieth century, Big Foot stories have been told on the radio and on television. He has appeared in numerous Hollywood films, sometimes as a terrifying bogeyman, more usually in recent years, in cheerful fantasy comedies, not to be taken too seriously. Now, in the twenty-first century, the Internet is the place to find all the information on the latest Big Foot sightings.

Though separated by many decades and hundreds of miles, the stories eye witnesses tell contain many of the same elements. The person is alone. It is night or dusk and visibility is poor. The sighting is as sudden as it is unexpected and usually lasts a matter of moments.

Doug Jamieson's story is typical. Now he's retired, but that night in 1987 he was driving home from the night shift at the factory where he worked. It was around midnight and his way home took him through the mountains of northern Oregon. Alone in the car and doing around 45 mph, eager no doubt to be home, Doug rounded a bend and found a Big Foot in the middle of the road. He says: 'It was big. It was furry. Standing straight up, with fir boughs under its right arm. I figured he's close to 7 feet [2m 15cm] tall and 250, 300 pounds [113–136kg] plus.'

Flabbergasted and scared, with the hair standing up

on the back of his neck, Doug put his headlights on full beam and saw a monkey-like creature, covered in hair except for its paler face. Within moments the creature was across the road and had disappeared down the hill, dragging its fir branches with it, going – Doug Jamieson guessed – to make its bed.

Though the encounter was brief, Doug is confident that this was not a case of mistaken identity. As a hunter, he's used to seeing the animals that roam the wild country of America's Pacific north-west.

'I've hunted for years. I know brown bears, black bears, elk ... and this was standing upright on two legs.'

Property services manager, Brian Smith's first encounter with Big Foot was similar. In the late 1980s he had moved up from Houston – far from Big Foot's stamping ground – to Walla Walla in the east of Washington State, which has over the past couple of decades gained something of a reputation for Big Foot sightings. He was out exploring, driving around the wild woods in his father's car. Like Doug, he was quite alone. On this occasion, though, it was daylight. He remembers: 'I came round the corner and had two Sasquatch come out of the woods and walk right across the road in front of me. One was approximately 6½, 7 foot [1m 80cm–2m 15cm] tall. The other one was 8 (foot) [2m 50cm]. The tall one was a dark brown colour. (The) smaller was a buckskin colour ... (They) were extremely well built animals. Very healthy, very human-looking. A very ape appearance.'

Though many witnesses say that the Big Foot was

surprised or scared, Brian Smith's two creatures apparently took his appearance calmly: 'They were very casual. They didn't seem threatened by me or spooked by me at all. They just walked right out and looked straight at me, minding their own business, and walked right across the road.'

For many years he never told anyone that they were not only very casual, they were also holding hands. But since then he has learnt from a primate expert that – assuming Big Foot to be a great ape – the fact that they were holding hands makes his sighting more credible rather than less so. Chimpanzees, for instance, like humans, hold hands. His second sighting was in October 2001. By then he was very much a part of the club of Big Foot enthusiasts, a self-confessed Sasquatch investigator and true believer. It was night and as this Big Foot crossed the road in the beam of Brian's headlights, another vehicle approached from the other direction. For a Sasquatch Investigator, this coincidence made it almost the perfect sighting: one Sasquatch seen by two independent groups of people simultaneously. Like Brian, the driver of this car too screeched to a halt. Brian got out of his car. The other people got out of theirs. As the Sasquatch disappeared off the road, Brian quickly approached the other witnesses hoping to compare notes. But this is America: as Brian approached the other car, the driver put his foot down and accelerated off into the night.

Frustrated and disappointed, Brian fetched his spotlight from the car and searched and searched, but he didn't catch sight of the Big Foot again. The next day he returned to the scene and again found nothing. No footprints, no dung, no hairs. No sign that a Big Foot had ever passed that way.

Apart from those people who glimpse Big Foot from their cars, the next most common category of eye witness is huntsmen. Unlike many of the typical drive-by eye witnesses, these men – and it is nearly always men – who catch sight of something that simply does not fit the pattern of those animals known to inhabit the north-west of North America certainly know their fauna.

Richard Ritchey lives near Portland, Oregon. He earns his living breeding snakes and lizards, which he shows on educational tours of local schools. On the side of his van is emblazoned his logo: the Reptile Man. But that day he was off-duty, out with his cousin, deer hunting with bow and arrow in the mountains. Dusk was falling. His cousin was a distance away when Richard, dressed in full camouflage and sitting in a hole he had made in the centre of a bush, heard the crashing of a large animal coming down the hill towards him. It was now about five minutes off being too dark to see, but as the noise came closer he saw that it was not an aggressive buck deer as he had thought. Not at all. It was a Big Foot. Nearly 2m 15cm tall and covered in 10cm-long hair, it came straight towards him, then stopped about 23 metres off.

According to Richard, the animal had: 'Definite wide shoulders. Definite big black hair hanging all over its whole body. Not really any facial expressions, except I could see a slight glint of eyes, and that's about it.'

Though he was so well concealed that another hunter could have come by within three metres and not have noticed him, Richard is sure that the creature knew he was there. It took a long look at him – hidden in his bush – and then turned and went back up the hill again. Though he has never seen one before nor since, Richard is now certain that Big Foot is out there. He says: 'There's over 90 planes that are actually missing, have crashed in the Cascade Mountain range and never been found … If you can lose a plane, you can lose a Big Foot very easily.'

He doesn't expect to see one again but this brief encounter, though it lasted less than a minute, was something very special – an experience he treasures. And – like Doug and Brian – he is happy to swear that he had been neither drinking nor taking drugs at the time.

Like most people who believe they have seen a Big Foot, he has met plenty of scepticism from those to whom he has told his story. Indeed, he's now so tired of the reaction that he rarely mentions his encounter in the forest. The night *he* glimpsed Big Foot, Doug Jamieson drove home and immediately woke up his wife. She didn't believe him, he admits. But Doug himself spent a sleepless night mulling over the sight of the huge creature crossing the road. He *knew* what he had seen. Since then, he's experienced the full range of reactions from friends and acquaintances. Some act as if he has gone mad. Others are inquisitive and want to know more. Others still assume it's simply a tall story and enjoy it as that.

Glimpses, brief encounters, shadows in the half-light of the evening, these are the typical Big Foot sightings. But some of the eye-witness evidence that the beast really does exist is much harder to explain away. And much more unsettling.

Tom Sewid lives on Vancouver Island, off the coast of the far western Canadian province of British Columbia. It's a huge forested island, about one and a half times the size of Wales, with the population of Cornwall. A sprinkling of towns and villages hug the shoreline but inland it is mostly a wilderness of old-growth forests. Tom's a keen hunter and he's a man who knows this forest and its wildlife well. He's a tracker who can identify an animal or a bird as much by its cries and the tracks it leaves behind as by what it looks like. For hundreds of years before white settlers reached here, this was home to a large number of indigenous tribal peoples. One of them was called the Kwakwaka'wakw – Tom Sewid's ancestors.

Tom was raised on stories about the Sasquatch. The male was known as Buquis – the wild man of the woods. The female was called Johnaquaha, and she was a terrifying, hairy creature who lived in an invisible home deep in the forests and craved human meat. Amongst the Kwakwaka'wakw, children were warned that the disobedient would be snatched by Johnaquaha and carried off to be killed. She was a kind of bogeyman.

Ironically, Johnaquaha was also one of the most coveted of all the family crests and carved on many of the island's wooden memorials that people mistakenly call totem poles. She can often be found in the most important place on the pole, the bottom, bearing the weight of everything higher up the pole. All his life Tom had heard the stories and seen Johnaquaha's image carved in wood and on rock. But he had always believed the Sasquatch was a mythical creature, until one evening in 1994. He says: 'I believe in him now. I have no doubt about it ... The old people are right ... They were recording something that truly is out there.'

At that time, Tom was the captain of a commercial salmon fishing boat. It was autumn and the weather was so lovely that he decided to take the boat, his girl-friend and the crew up to the north of Vancouver Island to the place of his ancestral home village. They had spent the day picking fruit from the abandoned trees in what had once been the village orchard, and catching crabs. Now it was evening and the boat was at anchor in a beautiful natural harbour where dark pine trees came down to a wide pebble beach. While Tom's girl-friend played cards with the engineer in the cabin, Tom and his crewman, Dean, were sitting on deck, minding a big bucket of crabs that was stewing on a propane stove. All around them it was absolutely quiet, the only sound coming from the music on the tape player in the cabin below.

It had been dark for about an hour and Tom and Dean were chatting and smoking when they were surprised to hear a sudden noise, as if something had been thrown against the metal side of an old trailer that had been left parked on the shore, about 200 metres away. To Tom, the sound was a confirmation of what in his heart he had already guessed, for there was a strange but distinctive smell in the air. Then came an unmistakable chirping, whistling sound. Tom and Dean – who is also a First Nation Canadian – exchanged glances. They were both sure that a Big Foot was out there.

Tom shouted to his girlfriend to turn off the music, and she and the engineer joined Tom and Dean on deck. They stood there together, their eyes becoming accustomed to the darkness, watching shadows moving on the beach. Then the whistling sound came again – much louder this time. The engineer threw his cigarette overboard and disappeared below decks, not to reappear again that night. But the other three crowded together, eager to get a better look. Tom adjusted the spotlight on the wheel house so it was pointing up the beach and switched it on. He remembers: 'There on the beach we saw two of them. The big one just dropped on his knee and pulled his arm up in front of his face. The one that was a little bit lower down and smaller – the female – dropped on its knees and went into a foetal position … The eyes were reflecting the light. They were green, greenish-yellow from the male with his arm up. You could see his arm moving because it would go one eye, two eyes, one eye … you could tell his arm was moving.'

Tom and Dean grabbed their guns and then stood there on the deck, gun barrels resting on the railing of the boat, pointing their guns at the two creatures on the beach. But the Sasquatch were too far away and the guns were not good enough to be certain of a successful shot at such a large and powerful creature at that range, in the spotlight. In any case, Tom's girl-friend – mindful of all the Quakwackywack legends that told of curses befalling those who harmed a Sasquatch – was urging them not to shoot. Slowly, the two men lowered their guns and then turned off the spotlight to save the old boat's battery. They went on standing there on deck, in the darkness, listening to the sounds of the two huge creatures moving about on the beach. Tom recalls: 'You could hear them going through the bush. Not like a bear that goes Crash! through the bush. Or a deer that goes Crash! Kerbunk! Crash! Or a wolf that makes that scattering noise, like a dog. This was something distinctively like a man who doesn't really want to make too much noise walking through the bush. You could hear that Swoosh!

Swoosh! and the branches being moved. And all of a sudden we just heard this noise like when you're walking in the forest and you put (your) hand against a rotten tree ... and it gives way. You hear that rotten wood sound as it caves in. We distinctly heard that.'

Then quietness fell across the remote bay again. It was a very still night, moonlit with good visibility, and sounds carried well. Though Tom strained his ears, he could hear nothing now. So he decided to start the boat's engine and recharge the battery. An hour and a half later, he shut the engine down again and the three of them came back up on deck, listening.

Suddenly there was a wild cry – the Whaa! Whaa! Whaa! of a blue heron that had been disturbed. It flew by Tom's boat, and then he heard something moving on the beach again. The boat was moored sideways on to the beach about a hundred yards off shore. Tom raked the shore with the spotlight and after 20 minutes or so, he and Dean caught sight of the Sasquatch for the second time. It was moving down the beach towards them, hiding behind rocks, reappearing, creeping, disappearing into the bush again. Closing in on them.

Tom recalls: 'And then, that's when Dean goes: "What the beep is that?" And that thing stood up. To this day I remember when it was stood up. You could see the hair hanging off its arm as it strolled. It made about six strides and it disappeared into the bush. Then we ran to the wheel house and hit the spotlight again, and we just could see the back part of it, as it was disappearing into the bushes. That's when I realised how big that thing was.'

Tom remembers how its arms hung much longer than a human's and how its neat, kempt hair – like a wolf's or a cougar's – was a light tan colour. It had a bouncing gait and the massive physique of the strongmen Tom recalls seeing on TV flipping over logs and tractor tyres. Nothing could have looked to his eyes less like a man dressed up in a monkey suit – this creature was streamlined and impressively sleek. But it disappeared into the forest, leaving Tom and his companions with an unforgettable memory and a sense of awe. He says: 'People ask me, "Were you scared?" I ain't gonna lie. It was pretty intimidating … Because, as a hunter who stalks animals, I was being stalked by it … I personally would never want to see it again unless I had a gun. It's intimidating.'

Since that day in 1994, Tom has talked to all kinds of people on the island about what he saw. It doesn't bother him that scientists dismiss Big Foot as a legend and the general public scoffs. He knows what he saw and in his experience, half of the loggers – the people who spend most time in British Columbia's forests – will admit in private that they too have seen the Sasquatch.

If stories like these were the sole evidence for the existence of an uncatalogued large creature in north-western North America, then few people – apart from the eye witnesses themselves – would be convinced.

But gradually over the years a wealth of other evidence has been accumulating, too.

Dr John Bindernagel is a Canadian wildlife biologist. He's a softly spoken man with a bushy beard and a very gentle manner. Now retired, he lives on Vancouver Island and devotes much of his time to trying to inject scientific method into the search for the elusive Sasquatch. After gathering evidence about this creature for more than a quarter of a century, these days he is much less interested in debating whether it exists than in trying to find answers to the kinds of questions zoologists normally ask in their regular fieldwork. How does the animal survive the winter? What is its diet? What is the typical family group? In other words, he starts from a position of belief and fits the evidence into that.

But what frustrates him is that the antagonism of his fellow professionals to Sasquatch research, and the scepticism of the media means that he is denied much of the evidence that he is sure is out there. He knows from experience that people are afraid of being ridiculed. Many simply never report what they have found or seen. He says: 'Although sightings are uncommon, I don't think they're nearly as uncommon as most of us have come to believe. I'm getting quite familiar with the problems that people have bringing forward a report ... I think many more people see them than people like me hear about, but they just don't want to talk about it. It's still not a safe subject to talk about, and I guess what I'm trying to do is help make it more of a safe subject. It's not only OK to have seen a Sasquatch, it's good … These are good wildlife sightings and people should be congratulated for them.'

He recalls one couple who were driving along in a car and saw a Sasquatch hauling a dead deer up a hillside. Neither of them said anything until 10 minutes later when they were many miles away and the husband turned to his wife and said, 'Did you see what I saw?' Seeing something that is *not supposed to exist* can be a terrible burden that leads some eye witnesses to need therapy and others to a lifetime of silence as if they have broken a taboo.

The closed minds of zoologists cause Bindernagel even greater anger. He recalls offering a paper on his research to a professional conference and being told that as long as Big Foot was the subject of tabloid headlines it would not be considered a suitable subject for a conference paper. He says: 'The problem isn't just that we don't recognise … (the existence of Big Foot); we are unwilling to examine the evidence, and that's what I find so distressing … It requires a certain humility for us to recognise that we may not know quite as much as we think we know about what is in our own forest here in North America.'

Bindernagel is tireless in the collection of evidence and approaches every story with an open mind. He frequently goes to meet people who have seen Big Foot or have found other evidence of its passing. Making a judgement as to their reliability as observers of forest life, he makes notes on what they have seen. Many spontaneously start to draw the creature they saw or describe its behaviour, and when some of the characteristics that have become familiar to him emerge, Bindernagel admits to feeling excited. Over and over again he is told about an upright human-like creature, covered in hair. People often refer to the animal's very long arms and its short thick neck, which gives it the appearance of a hunched American football player. The hair colour reported varies from dark brown to reddish brown and even white. Bindernagel is particularly struck by the similarities in small things: 'People notice ... the colour of the fingernails, copper coloured ... and the eye sockets and brow ridges. Absence of ears is interesting – Not the pointed ears of a bear ... Usually there's hair covering the ears, so I'm assuming they're very human-like but covered with hair. Every once in a while you get a difference in skull shape, usually not quite as flat as a human, often rounded like an ape, conical, even pointed.'

Eye witnesses also comment on Sasquatch's strange gait – so fluid and graceful and so unlike the gait of a human. Bindernagel is also struck by the way Big Foot's reported behaviour often fits a recognised pattern, too. This is an animal that throws chunks of wood, twists and snaps off tree branches, beats its chest and in many ways behaves just like a great ape.

And after so many years gathering the evidence,

that's precisely what Bindernagel believes the Sasquatch is – North America's great ape.

When he hears of a sighting, Bindernagel immediately goes to the place where it happened. Like a detective checking out the scene of the crime, he sets to work trying to understand the location from the point of view of a large primate. Why would the Sasquatch be there in the first place? Is it a likely habitat for such a creature could survive in? Does its presence there fit with the behaviour patterns Bindernagel is coming to recognise?

Frequently the sighting is made by a salmon river or on a beach where the Sasquatch could catch clams. There might be berries ripening on the bushes, or roots to dig for. Deer and squirrels could provide a source of meat. He can list more than 40 food sources readily available in the Pacific north-west of North America that would provide a great ape with sustenance.

Bindernagel believes from his researches that the Sasquatch is an elusive and shy animal that stays in the remotest forest. Often the creature is glimpsed in areas of secondary forest where the majestic ancient trees have been logged. As he comes to a better understanding of the Sasquatches' way of life and how they interact with the environment, Bindernagel now believes that those glimpsed in such areas are simply passing through on their way to less disturbed forests.

Altogether he has assembled a database of some 3,000 recent sightings, because of the embarrassment and fear of ridicule that so many people feel, in his opinion those 3,000 represent only the tip of the iceberg. He believes only one in a hundred sightings is ever reported.

But as a wildlife biologist Bindernagel is looking for much more than sightings, and the evidence he has examined over the years goes beyond the many credible eye-witness accounts. He has detailed physical evidence that he believes has been left by Big Foot – exactly the kind of evidence that he would compile in wildlife surveys for other animals in the forests of British Columbia. This evidence includes Sasquatch dung, which is described as being ropelike, unlike bear dung and occurring in such large quantities that it is difficult to know which other animal could have left it. He has collected notes on well concealed bedding sites and dens that are quite unlike those made by bears. They generally consist of a large circle of soft branches with a comfortable padding of ferns, moss and leaves, sometimes up to 15cm thick. Some appear to have been used over a period of time, as the top layer of leaves is fresh while the bottom has disintegrated to dust. Others have been found in caves or abandoned mine shafts. Bindernagel has even collected accounts of nests with some kind of a roof. Nest building is common to all the apes except for the gibbon, so it would be perfectly logical for North America's great ape to build such a nest, too.

He has collected evidence of 'twist off': branches up

to 10cm in diameter that have been twisted off trees about 1m 80cm from the ground. It's hard to think of a mechanical device capable of doing this and it would certainly be beyond the strength of man. These twisted off branches have been found near Big Foot sightings. One appeared still to have a hand print on it and had a strong smell.

He hopes one day to find a Big Foot body or skeleton, for this would be the incontrovertible proof that no one could deny. But he is not surprised that nothing has so far been found. In three decades of doing wildlife surveys in the forests he has only ever found two bear skulls, and he only found them because he trod on them by accident. Animal carcasses are quickly stripped and scattered by scavengers. The bones disintegrate in the acid soil.

But of all the evidence, the kind that he finds the most compelling is the tracks, and the casts made of these footprints. He says: 'I mean this is something very close to physical evidence. Something made those impressions in the soil. By casting them, we now have an impression of the bottom of the foot that made them. We have this remarkable consistency in the Sasquatch tracks across north America. Now I guess we have about 30 years worth of these ... and they keep appearing every year.'

Bindernagel has combined all this evidence in a book about America's missing great ape. He'd like visitors to the back country to see it as a field guide that can help them understand the strange evidence they might find and the strange creature they just might catch a glimpse of that no other North American field guides mention. But being a Sasquatch true believer is not without its personal cost. As he is the first to admit, to many people – to most people probably – believing in Big Foot is akin to believing in flying saucers. After 25 years of research, John Bindernagel has started to spend less time on the Big Foot trail and more time fishing and cross country skiing. He says: 'A few years ago someone asked me how long I'd been obsessed with the Sasquatch. I said, "I'm sorry. I thought you said *obsessed*." He said, "Yes, I did." I said, "Oh dear, I really didn't think I was, or if I was I didn't think it showed." But that made me think that maybe I should be backing off a little bit because obviously I was sounding obsessed and it is a problem.'

Though most are not as qualified as he is, there is no shortage of recruits to the army of Big Foot investigators ready to take his place and keep piling up the evidence.

Brian Smith's first encounter with Big Foot left him feeling exhilarated and special, as if singled out in some way for such an unusual experience. It gave him a new interest that he has pursued doggedly ever since. His wife, too, was disbelieving at first, until – camping in the mountains one night – she heard the eerie sound of the Sasquatch call nearby. It was night and Brian was off on his nightly search for Big Foot. To her horror she saw the shadow of some great beast making its way around the camping ground, running its hand along the outside of her tent. Now she too is a believer.

Brian Smith cheerfully admits to being obsessed. Three, four, five times a week he's out driving along the mountain roads of eastern Washington State searching for evidence. He says: 'My sightings inspired me to get into it because I saw a creature that's not supposed to exist and that can give you a lot of drive to get out there and look for the proof ... You become obsessed with getting to the bottom of it.'

He's convinced that a combination of time, the systematic attitude that the new generation of Big Foot enthusiasts have brought to the search and new technology will track Big Foot down. And soon. There is very little film or video evidence of the Sasquatch, and what there is, is fiercely contested. Brian is not surprised that it has proved so difficult to capture the creature on camera. It's a fast-moving and shy animal. Though he dreams of being the one who does manage to be in the right place at the right time, with his video camera at the ready, for the moment he is trying to tilt the odds in his favour by using new technology. He has set up cam trackers – cameras triggered by movement – in places where Sasquatch have been sighted. He puts bait, like a fresh salmon or some fruit, around 6 metres away from the camera in the hope that a Sasquatch will be tempted by the food and will then be caught on camera. He's also tried baiting the cam trackers with bright orange plastic chips, soaked in the powerfully smelling hormones of a female primate, in the hoping of attracting a male. As many anecdotes suggest Big Foot are interested in the sound of children laughing, he has tried taping a plastic doll that laughs 24 hours a day to a tree, too. But thus far Brian's efforts have been completely unsuccessful. His cam trackers have captured hikers and Girl Scouts, deer and even a cougar. But not a whisker of a Big Foot.

At night he goes out searching with thermal imaging cameras and state-of-the-art night vision binoculars called third-generation star scopes. He even broadcasts sounds recorded in the Californian mountains some years ago that some believe are authentic Sasquatch calls in the hope of getting a response. Sound travels better at night and most people believe Big Foot is nocturnal. But so far only coyotes have answered him.

Brian Smith is one of an army of volunteers for the BFRO (the Big Foot Research Organization). As well as depending on the energy and enthusiasm of its members, the organisation is trying to use computers to inject more scientific method into the search for Big Foot. Researcher Tom Powell, who runs the organisation's website, believes that the use of computers will soon transform Big Foot research: by giving researchers access to data, by enabling researchers to follow up quickly on sightings and by enabling researchers to track Big Foot remotely by the use of cameras in the field. The website is a forum for Big Foot sightings. Where once people's observations might have circulated among friends and family, now they can be centrally collated within hours of the sighting and shared with the community of Big Foot enthusiasts.

Once the BFRO is told of a sighting, an investigator like Brian Smith can be dispatched to the scene. Brian frequently goes to meet people in his part of America's Pacific north-west, who think they may have seen Big Foot. He makes a detailed study of the story itself and the location, covering every inch of the ground in search of broken branches, tracks or dung. In his experience, the swift-footed creature is often seen for as little as three seconds – and a good half of those who claim to have seen something are probably mistaken. There are plenty of hoaxers around, too.

He passes on the details to researchers like Tom Powell, who believes they now have so much data that they are easily able to distinguish between credible and unlikely stories. The details of the credible ones are entered into the database, and an artist uses them to make a sketch of what was described. The BFRO website now contains a veritable rogues' gallery of Big Foots – of almost every shape and size. Their very variety is what interests Tom Powell. He says: 'We have a virtual police line-up of Big Foot sketches which shows us that they are of wildly variable appearances. They are very individual in their appearances and …

it's a very interesting combination of human and animal features. They certainly show in their faces a personality that is seldom seen in animals.'

Thus far, there is little filmed evidence of Big Foot. From his experience, this doesn't surprise Brian. With Big Foot's perfect camouflage, its nocturnal and shy behaviour and the speed at which it moves, to get clear footage would be little short of miraculous. But Brian's not the only one to have set up cameras in likely locations, hoping to capture Big Foot. Tom Powell is cautiously optimistic about the BFRO's experiments: 'We are getting mildly encouraging results so far. The project is in its infancy. We have some interesting shapes and images that hint that the animals are there. We haven't yet gotten pictures that we're eager to put before the public but we'll keep working on this project and we hope to find more locations through some sort of publication of our effort. So the website is giving us a way to let people know what we're doing.'

For Tom, the computer is Big Foot's best friend for it will soon prove the creature's existence. Or, he adds thoughtfully, if Big Foot is trying to stay hidden, it will turn out to be his greatest enemy.

Brian Smith's lack of success thus far has not discouraged him: 'Sasquatch research investigation is very, very addictive. You'll sit up every night of the week … You're out here in the pitch black. You're looking for a monster, and you can spook yourself very easily hearing a branch break in the wind or an elk jump out from behind you. It can be scary. But it's fun.'

Another obsessive is Paul Freeman. He's spent whole summers out in the woods just hoping to catch sight of Big Foot. One summer he spent a total of 4,000 hours on watch, just coming back to civilisation when he ran out of groceries. He was, he says, 'hooked on it like some people are hooked on fishing'. In his time he's seen thousands of footprints and five actual creatures. He's also seen all kinds of violent evidence – trees uprooted and laid across trails, cougars with their heads torn off – that he attributes to Big Foot. He's heard noises that he knows are Big Foot – a screeching like a woman or a peacock – and smelled Big Foot's sickeningly strong odour. He once found some dung that he dried out and sent to Scotland Yard for identification, but he never heard anything back.

After 15 years of chasing and observing, Freeman has drawn up a map of his area and worked out where Big Foot are likely to be at each season. This is the reason, he believes, why he has been so much more successful than other Big Foot enthusiasts. For years he packed a gun, and then he stopped seeing them. But when he left his gun behind and took a video camera instead, then he started seeing them again. He wonders if they have some sixth sense. Indeed, all his encounters have left him with a healthy respect for the beast. He says: 'They seem like they know everything you're doing when you're up there. Those things are intelligent. A hell of a lot smarter than we give them (credit for) you know. They've been here a long time and they'll be here a long time after we're gone.'

He even managed to shoot a lengthy video of what he says is a genuine Sasquatch moving through the woods.

The evidence gathered by enthusiasts and amateurs – and by the obsessives – is now being seriously considered by a handful of scientists, respected in their different fields. Dr Henner Fahrenbach is a primate expert and statistician who first came across Big Foot because the institute where he worked used to be sent samples of so-called Big Foot hairs for analysis. As a keen hiker, he has no problem believing that there could be unknown creatures hiding out in the remaining wilderness areas of North America. But what really made him take the possibility seriously was the statistical survey that he undertook of the evidence that he agrees with Dr John Bindernagel is the most compelling: the footprints.

Over the years, Fahrenbach discovered, the casts of footprints had been collected – 'like stamps' – but nothing had been done with them. He made a statistical analysis of their length and graphed it out. What emerged was a graph that made the classic bell-shaped curve of a true living population. In other words, there were a few footprints that were smaller than average and a few that were larger than average, but the great majority fell in the middle of the graph. It was the kind of pattern that he would expect if he had made a graph of a random sample of human foot size, or weight, or arm reach. These Big Foot footprints had been collected over 40 or 50 years, from all over north and west America. If they were the product of half a century of hoaxers, Fahrenbach explains, the graph would not have shown the normal distribution that produces a bell-shaped curve but would have shown a scattering of sizes, for the different hoaxers would all have made hoaxed tracks of random sizes.

Fahrenbach has also analysed hairs that people hope can be attributed to Big Foot. As something of an expert in the analysis of hairs, Fahrenbach is not easily persuaded. Over the years he has dismissed all manner of hairs brought in by the credulous. The key element of the hair to analyse is the medulla. He explains: 'To differentiate Sasquatch hair from the hair (of) other animals in the forest is relatively simple. All the carnivores have very crisp medullas with blocky cells ... Deer, elk, moose have hair that looks like styrofoam. Rodents have hair that is very characteristic. Really the only hair that Sasquatch hair – to my judgment – at this point can be confused with is human hair ... We don't have other primates running around in the forest.'

Thus far Fahrenbach has obtained 15 samples of hair, collected by different people from different places over a number of years. All these samples look the same. One is about 10cm long and shows no evidence of ever having been cut. He is convinced that these are 15 samples of Sasquatch hair. But no laboratory has yet managed to extract sufficient DNA from a sample to sequence a gene. So proof – one way or the other – still eludes the Big Foot believers.

Over the years, many thousands of people have seen some evidence of Big Foot. But many millions have seen the most famous evidence of all: the film footage shot on 20 October 1967 by two Big Foot hunters, Bob Gimlin and Roger Patterson. It runs for 8 seconds, in a slightly washed-out colour, and shows a dark-haired apelike creature crossing a sandy stretch of ground on the edge of forest in California. Patterson and Gimlin were riding on horseback at Bluff Creek that day, specifically hoping to catch Big Foot on camera. As they came round a bend, they spotted the creature crouching by the river.

Patterson later described how his horse reared up at the sight of the Big Foot and threw him, but he was able to grab his camera and film for a few moments, capturing the creature clearly. As it lopes away, the giant ape turns briefly back towards the camera, and as it turns its breasts swing into view, suggesting that this is a female Sasquatch. Patterson took casts of the tracks supposedly left by the creature he had filmed. Russian cryptozoology experts analysed the footage in the late 1960s and declared it authentic. Because it was shot on film, every frame can be enlarged without loss of quality and every frame has indeed been pored over and argued over without anyone being able to settle the issue conclusively.

For Fahrenbach, there is no question about its authenticity: 'The question always comes up, what about the Patterson movie? It is simply the real thing. And they were just extremely lucky to be at the right place at the right time with the right equipment ... We have a footprint of the creature. We have the step length of the creature. From computer analysis we know exactly how tall it was ... (The creature on the film is) a little below the mean of a population in size and footprint length, so there's really no reason to doubt it ... Patterson himself never really made much money out of it. He could have gotten his money and run, but he pumped it all back into research and died of cancer very shortly thereafter, so the behaviour pattern of the observer did not smack of a spoof or a fabrication. Besides that, the creature has ... a very fluid gait, very smooth, and it is impossible for a human to imitate that gait. You just put a suit on and try it and people are going to be laughing at the feeble effort. It's not possible to make a convincing copy of the Sasquatch walk because it's a different gait.'

Dr Fahrenbach is not the only reputable scientist who finds the footage authentic. Professor Jeff Meldrum is an anatomist from the Department of Biological Sciences at Idaho State University. He views the Patterson-Gimlin footage with an eye to the creature's anatomy and he is convinced: 'I find it extremely compelling because the features of the foot that I have investigated and documented in numerous examples of footprint casts are vividly exhibited on the Patterson film.'

He also finds it chimes with what eye witnesses say about the way the animal moves: 'Many eye witnesses comment on an apparent gliding motion evidenced in these animals. I've had one eye witness comment it looked like they were riding on roller skates, or another that they were actually floating in the air, because there was this very evident lack of a head bob that's characteristic of a more stiff-legged human gait. And this also speaks to this bent-kneed posture the film subject on the Patterson film exhibits. It is this very same type of dynamic. It moves very smoothly, very fluidly and with a forward lean of the shoulders and head and clearly with bent hips and bent knees ...'

But it was not the famous footage that convinced Jeff Meldrum that Big Foot is not just a large figment of the American imagination. He has made the most systematic analysis ever of the Big Foot feet. In drawers at his laboratory, he has a collection of over 100 casts of footprints and more than 50 photographs of footprints purporting to be of Big Foot. His interest in the subject dates from one day in 1996. He had gone to see the enthusiast and multiple Big Foot eye witness Paul Freeman at his home in Walla Walla, eastern Washington state. To his delight, Freeman was able to take him out immediately to see some fresh Big Foot tracks.

The footprints were 35 centimetres long and 13 centimetres wide, and the track went on for around 50 yards. Meldrum was immediately struck by the way the footprints varied slightly, depending on the ground. For him, seeing was believing. What convinced him was the way the prints interacted with the ground they were going across, showing a splaying, a stretching and then a curling of the toes, a flexion of the foot and signs of slippage in the wet. To someone familiar with footprints, as he is, these were all indications that this was a living track and not the activities of a hoaxer.

However, this was the only occasion when he was lucky enough to be in the right place at the right time and see fresh tracks in the ground. As he admits, it's not possible to study the Big Foot phenomenon under controlled conditions and he is 'at the mercy of the good fortune of witnesses and would be investigators'. Now he actively collects casts of prints, encouraging people to send them to him for examination. This analysis is producing results: 'What is emerging is a very consistent and yet distinct anatomy of the foot that characterises these tracks and is very consistent with the reported habits, manner of walking, and habitat in which these animals reportedly live.'

The casts of the footprints in his laboratory in Idaho are mostly very large and, to the eye of a lay person, unconvincing in their flatness – they seem indeed like the cartoon feet of a larger than life human. But Meldrum is looking for something quite specific in the casts. He says: 'We look for things like repeat appearances of individuals at given localities. We look for variation in toe position from one footprint to another. We look for consistency in the anatomy: do the toes articulate with the foot? Are they jointed in a reasonable fashion? Does the foot interact in a dynamic way with the ground that the individual is travelling over?'

What is emerging is a pattern that he feels is consistent. The foot is broad in comparison to its length. The heel is elongated and the toes are relatively big. It has no arch like a human foot. Nor does it share any characteristics with known North American animals like bears. To him, there are only two explanations: it's a hoax or it's an unknown animal. No chance of a misidentification.

So how likely is it that this is a hoax?

Meldrum admits that he has come across many hoaxes. There are casts with a very odd arrangement of toes or an unlikely number. He has received copies of, supposedly original, casts that he already has. Indeed, recently he was sent a cast supposedly of a track a hunter had found, and it was a copy of a cast that he knows was made seven years before. But these hoaxes do not tell the whole story: 'After careful analysis of these numerous examples of footprint casts and seeing the consistency and yet the complexity of the foot anatomy that is evident here, it really is inconceivable that these could be made by some sort of contrived artifice,' he explains. 'I have essentially reached a point in this analysis where it's unreasonable to suggest that all of these tracks are hoaxed. Because who is orchestrating this? Who is co-ordinating the effort so that there's this consistent anatomy that crops up time and time and time again through time and space? It's more unreasonable and more outrageous in my mind to suggest that such a conspiracy exists than to acknowledge at least the possibility that these animals may in fact exist.'

As Meldrum admits, his work is not helped by the strange world that the Big Foot enthusiasts inhabit. Some of the self-appointed investigators clearly detest all others in the field and never let an opportunity go by to show all other investigators in a bad light. Many are very territorial and are quick to discredit anyone who strays onto their patch. Though some – as John Bindernagel has found – are depressed by the ridicule heaped upon them and keep very quiet about their hobby, others are hungry for the limelight and stoop quickly to embellishing the evidence or making it up entirely in the hope of gaining more publicity and attention. It's a difficult world for a scientist to operate in. More and more, he tries to rely on people like Brian Smith whom he has grown to trust over the years, and on physical evidence rather than eye-witness testimony. As he candidly admits:

'Eye-witness testimony is probably the least reliable and the least useful evidence in this research. You're just at the mercy of the credibility of the individual and their motivation. But more importantly and more fundamentally, you're at the mercy of the powers of observation of that individual, and without the appropriate training ... they often times misinterpret or misidentify ... If all we had were the eye witnesses this could easily be dismissed as nothing more than mass hysteria ... But imaginations don't leave footprints in the ground.'

Then one day Jeff Meldrum won an unlikely ally. Jimmy Chilcutt is a police officer from Conroe, which is just outside Houston, in Texas. For 14 years he has been a fingerprint examiner working as a Crime Scene Investigator. But he is not just an expert on human finger- and footprints – in the study of dermatoglyphics and dermoridges, as it is more correctly known.

Some years ago he became interested in seeing the differences between the prints of non-human primates. He visited a number of zoos and persuaded keepers to let him take prints of apes and chimpanzees. He is now one of the very few people in the world – perhaps the only one indeed – who has a working knowledge of both human and primate foot- and fingerprints.

He had never taken any interest in Big Foot, but watching TV at home one night he saw a programme in which Jeff Meldrum talked about his Big Foot casts. Jimmy Chilcutt realised that his unique expertise might be of use to the professor.

He travelled to Idaho, and initially, as Jeff Meldrum pulled the casts out of the many drawers for him to see, he was disappointed. Out of around 100 casts that he examined, only four or five actually showed dermaridges. But he was not surprised: 'The reason is because when you're casting a foot impression the soil has to be real fine. It has to be just perfect to pick up the dermaridges.'

But in these casts he was able to identify markings that were sufficiently similar to those on human and primate for him to be sure he was dealing with a real creature, with real big feet. What fascinates Chilcutt is not so much the similarities but the significant differences between these markings and those of other primates. In humans, dermaridges run straight across the foot; in other primates they run at an angle; but in these Big Foot casts they run lengthways along the foot. Such a subtle detail, he feels sure, is an unlikely one for a hoaxer to know about.

In his examination, he also found that two of the casts were identical: in his opinion clearly from the same Big Foot. And they showed not only that the creature had grown up in the intervening years, but that it had sustained wounds to its feet. He explains: 'The northern California cast that I examined first has the clearest dermaridges. This was a casting of a juvenile animal who was small. The Walla Walla cast was unique in the fact that it not only had the ridge flow going down the side of the foot, up and down the length of the foot, but it also had scars. And scars were significant in this investigation because in a human being when you cut your finger and the skin heals, the ridges curl inward during the healing process. I noticed the same phenomenon on the Walla Walla cast. Where this animal had been cut, as the wound healed, the ridges curled inward. It's a biological function of healing skin. The first cast from Northern California was made in 1967; 15 years later the Walla Walla cast was created and that's hundreds of miles away and years apart. Someone faking these would have to have been the same person, because the ridge characteristics, the texture and the ridge flow pattern are the same in both castings.'

After two years of examining prints, Jimmy Chilcutt does not mince his words: 'As a latent fingerprint examiner, it's my responsibility never to make a mistake, because when I give testimony in court, someone goes to jail. So I have to be extremely careful when I make a decision or when I make a statement … I approach the Big Foot situation with the same professionalism. And, after examining the prints, I think there is no possibility that they have been faked, and that it is definitely a primate that made the prints.'

Jimmy Chilcutt's support is satisfying for Jeff Meldrum. But it is not just the consistency of the tracks that make him a believer. He is also persuaded that the tracks – and the Patterson-Gimlin footage – suggest a plausible anatomy for a great ape living in the rough terrain of America's north-west. Humans were adapted for open countryside and endurance running. Our stiff-legged gait is appropriate for this. The massive, heavy Sasquatch lives in a very different habitat. Meldrum says: 'Walking with bent knees and bent hips allows them to navigate this very broken terrain in a much (more) efficient way. In fact when we don a heavy back-pack and try to walk over broken terrain, we naturally adopt the same kind of walk. We bend our knees to avoid the shock and the jolt of a stiff-legged heel strike, and it allows us to move through the step in a much smoother and more efficient way. They've maintained this more primitive way of walking on two legs – that of having bent knees, bent hips, mid-foot flexibility. (It) doesn't allow them to run a marathon, but they can hike up and down a mountainside much more efficiently than any human possibly could.'

So is the evidence that is stacking up beginning to make a believable case for the Sasquatch? Is it now more likely than ever that a previously unknown primate will soon be discovered living somewhere between the Pacific Ocean and the Rockies?

Dr Robin Crompton, Reader in Anatomy at the University of Liverpool does not think so. He is a world expert in the evolution of walking in primates and he takes issue with Jeff Meldrum's analysis on a number of grounds. Failing a specimen – alive or dead – Crompton finds the evidence put forward by Sasquatch enthusiasts so far simply unconvincing. The Patterson-Gimlin footage and the video footage shot by Paul

Freeman much more recently, for instance, to his mind simply fail the authenticity test. Though the Freeman footage shows a creature hidden amongst trees, the Patterson-Gimlin film gives a very clear view of the animal in bright light. However, as a scientist who routinely uses film as a tool to analyse anatomy and movement, Robin Crompton knows that extremely high-speed film is necessary to capture the nuances of bodies in motion. Film stock that shoots at 250 frames per second is needed. The Patterson-Gimlin footage was shot at only 25 frames per second.

Even taking the footage at face value, Crompton's analysis is crisp. Firstly, the proportions of the body are much more human than ape: 'The length of the arm is exactly the same as that of you or I. The relative length of the lower limb segments – the upper and lower leg – is the same as of you or I.'

Secondly, the creature is swinging its arms as it walks – one arm swinging forward at the same time as the leg on the other side. 'That's something that humans do; no ape does that at all,' says Crompton.

Thirdly, he explains, the body posture is illogical and goes against what anatomists know about locomotion. The knees are bent and with gravity tending to make the knees flex more, the natural tendency would be for the back to be bent forward. But the creature is walking with a relatively straight back: 'That makes no sense,' he says. 'The two don't go together as a natural realistic form for any animal.'

In fact this whole manner of walking is contradictory to all the research Dr Crompton has done. He says, 'The creature has the same proportions as a modern human, has the same body mass distribution as a modern human' and yet in spite of this, it has adopted a strange gait that is neither human nor truly ape-like. 'The walk with bent knees and a straight back is so difficult to sustain that it would cost it twice as much as walking upright.'

Experiments with chimpanzees, which do walk with bent knees, have shown that they can only go for a maximum of 20 paces upright before they fall back onto walking on all fours. They do not have the muscle power to maintain this bent-legged gait on two feet for long. Crompton concludes: 'I am afraid I just cannot accept that an animal could evolve for thousands of years, moving in that sort of a habitat ... and would yet have adopted a very expensive way of moving around. It's just not something which holds together.'

The creature in the Patterson-Gimlin film also turns back towards the camera at one point, and this gives Crompton another reason to doubt its authenticity. Apes have massive neck muscles compared to humans, and this gives them much less flexibility. When a chimp wants to look over its shoulder, it must turn its whole body. When a human needs to take a look behind, it need only turn its neck – and that's just what this Big Foot does.

Those who believe in Big Foot always explain the

lack of photographic evidence by explaining that the creature is both very swift-moving and extremely shy. To Crompton, the Patterson-Gimlin footage fails to fit this picture: 'This sequence does not show a shy animal. This animal is not running away at high speed from the photographer.' In the course of his work, he has followed shy animals around, trying to get footage for his research and in his experience they behave quite differently: 'I have actually followed animals around which have never been followed before, and, believe you me, they disappear an awful lot quicker than that did!' He says, 'I do have to conclude that the footage represents nothing more than a man walking in a gorilla suit.'

And if it *is* a man in a monkey suit then the strange way of walking makes every sense to Crompton, for it fits a rather old-fashioned view of the evolution of walking – a view that might have been current among the Big Foot hunting community of the 1960s when this footage was filmed: 'It's walking like that, I'm afraid, because it rather fits the kind of old-fashioned idea of how we learned to walk: that firstly we were quadrupeds and from being a quadruped to being a biped ... you inevitably must walk around in a crouched sort of way.'

But one hoaxed piece of footage – if that's what the Patterson-Gimlin film is – does not undermine all the other evidence. Crompton, however, is equally unimpressed by the casts of footprints. Ape footprints and human footprints show clear – yet distinct – patterns, matched to their different ways of walking. In chimpanzees and apes, the feet are mainly adapted for grasping. In humans, the feet are mainly adapted for walking upright. The Big Foot footprints show a mixture of both characteristics, and so they do not hold together. Crompton says, 'It is showing some of the most advanced features of the human foot while retaining the features of a chimpanzee's foot. It is such an unlikely combination that you just can't believe in it. The two things put together make no functional sense ... You have a posterior foot which is working like that of a chimpanzee and the front part of the foot which is working like that of a human.'

This says something to Crompton: it's a cast 'which has been made to look like something which is halfway between a human and a chimpanzee'.

Moreover, the casts he has been able to examine show the imprint of feet that are so different that, in his opinion, they simply could not belong to the same species. He is also unconvinced by Meldrum's assertion that the footprints are a living track. Crompton believes that a hoaxer could easily make his fake Big Foot foot slide, rock or make different depths of depression as necessary to make the track appear more realistic.

Another piece of evidence that is frequently cited by Big Foot investigators is an 80-minute recording of sounds, made in the high sierras of California in 1975.

It's a mixture of gruntings and snortings, whistling sounds and screams, recorded by a group of Big Foot hunters who baited an area of forest and dangled a microphone above the bait.

Dr David Chivers is an expert in primate sounds from Cambridge University. His particular area of expertise is Indonesia and he is a firm believer in 'Orang Pendek'. Like Big Foot, this is an ape that many people believe to exist but which has so far eluded capture, either in the flesh or on film. The evidence cited shares many similarities with that for Big Foot – sightings, some footprints, some hair, evidence of foraging and even some recorded sounds. Like Big Foot researchers, the Orang Pendek researchers have so far failed to extract DNA from the hair samples. But David Chivers believes this scant evidence adds up to a credible picture and he actively promotes research into Orang Pendek. So he is not unsympathetic to researchers struggling against a tide of scientific scepticism.

However, when *Incredible Stories* producer Tim Hopewell took the tape of sounds claimed to be Big Foot for him to analyse, he was totally flummoxed: 'It's very difficult to make serious scientific comment on this … I've never heard a recording of a wild animal like that. It's too close. There's no background noises … My immediate reaction is, you've got a couple of people in a bar late at night making odd noises. There's nothing really reminiscent of chimpanzees or gorillas or orangutans.'

He could identify only a very few sounds that reminded him of primate calls. But more importantly, the range of sounds was in his opinion impossible for any single creature to make. There were pig-like grunting noises and human-like sounds, almost like words being formed. There were whistlings. Though apes do imitate other animals' calls, such a wide repertoire of sounds is beyond a single animal. Unless that animal was a human.

The pattern of the sounds also did not make any sense to him. All animal calls have a structure and a coherence. They are, after all, a means of communication. The orangutan, for instance, has a particular long call. It goes on for five minutes but it has a clear internal logic. The sounds on the tape, Chivers explained, had no structure discernible and were merely a jumble of different noises. This is not the way animals use sound.

Though he is optimistic about the chances of researchers finding one 'missing' ape, Dr Chivers is much less sanguine about the Big Foot enthusiasts' chances of success. The Sumatran habitat where he believes the gibbon known as Orang Pendek may be hiding is extremely dense, offering both protection and plenty of food. The Pacific north-west is quite a different habitat.

Robin Crompton, too, thinks the inappropriateness of north-west America as a home for a primate is another strong reason against Big Foot existing anywhere except in people's imagination, quite apart from the unconvincing nature of the evidence. As a student of primates, he contends that there are good reasons *not* to expect to find a primate in North America. There are today no primates existing outside the tropics, apart from a Himalayan lemur and humans. He says, 'It is ... really not very likely that we're going to discover new primates in a habitat which is not classic primate habitat.'

The classic primate habitat is the tropical rainforest. And with good reason. Primates eat fruit, berries and in some rare cases meat. In the tropical forest, the rich diversity of plants provides an equally rich range of foods and so can support a large number of animals. In temperate regions like North America, by contrast, the range and quantity of food available drops enormously. Moreover, in North America a primate would be in direct competition with bears that are also foraging for these same foods. The competition for food would increase in winter time when food resources become even more scarce. Some Big Foot believers have suggested the creature might hibernate to survive the winter. But Crompton thinks this is unlikely. Higher primates cannot hibernate, as they are unable to lower their metabolic rate sufficiently for long periods.

But Professor Meldrum does not see this as a problem. So many sightings of Big Foot occur at night that he believes these are nocturnal animals, and so manage to avoid direct competition with bears by hunting and foraging at different times of day.

Robin Crompton disagrees. The cells in the eye are selected by evolution to be either better at seeing colour or better at seeing in the dark. All primates have evolved to be better at seeing colour – a great advantage for creatures that are fruit-eaters. If Big Foot manages to survive at night, then it must have reversed millions of years of primate evolution to develop eyes that are better at night sight. Though Crompton admits that evolution does sometimes reverse itself, to him 'the combination of being an ape – in other words an animal which eats fruit a large amount of the time – and being night-active is highly unlikely in itself.'

Taking all these factors into consideration, Crompton's objection to Big Foot is first and foremost as a scientist who believes the evidence is simply not good enough. Sightings, even if there are 3,000 of them, unidentified droppings, footprints, strange hairs, damaged foliage and nests in the woods are not enough: 'You have to have a real physical specimen before a species can be expected to exist. Science requires evidence of a real animal which can be measured, which can be observed, which can be compared by other people to existing species before we can recognise a previously unknown species as a real zoological species.'

He does not believe science has anything to lose by

discovering that there are new species out there. In the 1990s, three new species of lemur were identified in the forests of Madagascar and a new antelope was discovered in Vietnam. He says: 'It's not that we wish to exclude new species from recognition, because this happens all the time. It's simply that scientific standards have to be maintained … a footprint, a piece of hair, an observation even less, is just not acceptable.'

So why, given that all his instincts as a scientist and a student of primate behaviour tell him there is no possible truth in the Big Foot story, does Robin Crompton think some of his fellow scientists are true believers? He responds: 'I think … all of us like some excitement in our lives. Many people in this country are tempted to invest in the National Lottery knowing that they have a chance of one in a couple of million of getting the money. But all of us, however well trained we are in science, can occasionally persuade ourselves that, Yes, this time I really stand a chance. I'm going to win the lottery.'

And what about the army of enthusiasts and eye witnesses? Are they just unhinged? Crompton says: 'People have claimed to see bipedal animals several times. I've got to say that people have claimed to see flying saucers several times and, yes, these people who see the flying saucers and see the bipeds … are perfectly normal people like ourselves. Humans do have imaginations, and it is easy to make an object out of shadows in the forest. I think all of us know that. No one is saying that people are unreasonable for thinking that such creatures may exist.'

In fact, he blames scientists for the way such stories gain a foothold in the popular imagination. In his opinion, scientists like to stay hidden in their laboratories and generally do not spend enough time trying to communicate with the general public. Scientists would much rather speak to each other and so they leave the communication of scientific ideas to journalists and novelists. It's not surprising that journalists and novelists tend to pick upon ideas not in the mainstream but at the tantalising margins of science and scientific research.

Henner Fahrenbach puts professional lack of interest in Big Foot research in a different context. He believes scientists are too worried about taxpayers and grants committees: 'The average scientist worries about his job more than about the Sasquatch. I'm retired. I don't give a hoot what they think and my scientific reputation rests on other things than Sasquatch. Sasquatch is a hobby for me, so I don't have to really worry. But it is unusual that scientists who are ordinarily intensely curious about the unknown should shun this particular unknown.'

The last word is with Robin Crompton: 'It's not up to me or other scientists who are sceptical of these species to demonstrate that they don't exist. It is up to the scientists who do believe that they exist to prove to the rest of us that we're wrong.'

And thus far – websites and enthusiasts not with-standing – the majority of professional scientists remain unconvinced by the evidence that has been found.

The North American Sasquatch is not the only myste-rious outsize creature that people believe they have seen in remote places.

In Sumatra, the westernmost island of the Indonesian archipelago, local people talk of the Orang Pendek, a huge ape. A Dutch scientific research team in the 1920s believed they had found evidence of a primate that was not a gibbon. Recently a British research team has found footprints and hairs here, and the habitat is one that could certainly sustain a large primate. However, it has proved impossible to extract DNA from the hairs, possibly as a result of their strong red pigment.

In central China, researchers believe there may be 1,000 to 2,000 ape-like creatures who roam the forests, particularly in the Shennongjia Nature Reserve in Hubei province. Stories of such wild men of the woods and mountains date back 3,000 years in China. Evidence collected over the years, including sightings by local people, describe a creature that is over 1m 82cm, with reddish brown hair, long limbs and a strong and unpleasant smell. Footprints 40 centimetres long and corn cobs that had been strangely chewed were found by researchers at a spot where a hunter claimed to have seen the beast in 2000. Local people call it Ye Ren, which means Wild Man.

Researchers from China's Committee for Research into Strange and Rare Animals have made numerous research trips, even using remote sensing equipment deployed on hot air balloons to help them, but so far nothing concrete has been found.

In Russia there are also numerous accounts of a man-beast, sometimes known as the Alma, sometimes as the 'Russian Yeti'.

The Russians have a great deal of historical evidence – foot, hand and body prints: voice and hair samples: drawings and eye-witness reports. There are many eye-witness accounts of encounters with the Russian Yeti. In 1989 some men from the Ukraine captured a creature believed to be a Yeti. They held it for seven hours before it escaped.

Every month the Seminar of Relic Hominoids takes place at the Darwin Museum in Moscow. Scientists and experts from all over Russia and sometimes those from abroad come together to discuss new evidence and theories.

The Nepalese believe there are three different kinds of Yeti: a big one that is a man-eater, a man-size one that inhabits rocky areas, and a smaller one that lives in the jungle. In the 1950s and 60s, there were a number of British expeditions to the Himalayas. During these trips, a mummified hand, a scalp and various footprints were found. Hair from the scalp was analysed and thought to be primate hair. The thumb was brought back to England for analysis but was subsequently lost.

However, there have been few Yeti sightings in the Himalayas during the past 30 to 40 years: a man, now in his fifties, described seeing a female Yeti drinking water around 30 years ago, and around 40 years ago a tale was current of a young girl being attacked in a village. Many Nepalese believe the Yeti did exist but is now extinct.

Encounters with the Abominable Snowman, as the Yeti is also called, are something of the stock-in-trade of mountaineers. Many an expedition to the Himalayas has generated stories about mysteriously disappearing chocolate bars, or massive footprints in the snow, or strange shapes seen lumbering away across the snowfield. Some have blamed hypoxia, the condition of mental confusion caused by lack of oxygen to the brain at altitude. Massive footprints have been explained by the way the snow melts around footprints making them appear much larger than they really are.

But world-famous mountaineer Reinhold Messner's sighting, in 1986, of a strange creature that left massive footprints in black mud set him on a decade-long search for the Yeti. After travelling all over the Himalayas through Nepal and Tibet and talking to everyone from the Dalai Lama to nomadic yak herders, he became convinced that the origin of the legend was a rare mountain bear known as a chemo, glimpses of which had over generations been woven into the legend of the Yeti.

CHAPTER 2

The Curse of King Tutankhamun's Tomb

I t was the greatest find in archaeology of the twentieth century and perhaps of any century: the near perfect tomb of the boy king Tutankhamun, discovered by self-taught Egyptologist and adventurer Howard Carter in 1922.

But the lucky discovery that made Carter's career proved, it seems, disastrous for others who came in contact with the tomb. His patron, Lord Carnarvon, was dead within months. Other deaths and misfortunes followed.

Had the archaeologists triggered some curse – a powerful spell laid by the original builders of the tomb?

And if there was no curse, why did people die? And why did the story of the Curse of the Mummy's Tomb catch on so quickly and prove so enduring?

It is November 1922. Professional archaeological digger Howard Carter is excavating in Upper Egypt, financed – as he has been for nearly 15 years – by his wealthy patron, the collector and Egypt enthusiast, Lord Henry Carnarvon. But this season things are different, and Carter knows that he is in a race against time. Unless he can make a truly spectacular discovery this will be his last season under Carnarvon's sponsorship.

For the wealthy British aristocrat has decided to stop funding Carter. Their early archaeological successes, in the years before the Great War, have been followed by many lean years, when Carter has found almost nothing of value. Carnarvon has agreed to fund only one more season 'as a gambling man', after Carter himself offered to finance the 1922 season out of his own very meagre savings.

Carter returns to the Valley of the Kings, where he has been excavating without much success for more than seven years, and on 1 November begins to dig. Just four days later, on the morning of 5 November, he makes an amazing discovery. Under the remains of some workmen's huts, built to shelter the men who dug Ramesses VI's tomb more than 3,000 years ago, he finds a stone step buried some 4 metres below the surface of the valley floor. As he and his team of Egyptian excavators continue to dig down, they find 11 more steps leading steeply downwards. With mounting excitement, they then uncover the top of a doorway. The doorway is still plastered shut, the plastering stamped with large oval seals. The workmen's huts that had been built over this hidden doorway date from the twentieth Dynasty – around 1150 BC –

so Carter knows this tomb is earlier. He cannot decipher any name. But he *can* see something that he later admitted set his pulse racing: an impression of a seal, showing a jackal above nine kneeling captives. This is the royal necropolis seal – proof that the tomb's occupant is of very high status, probably a king. It's all Carter needs to see. He immediately gets his workmen to re-cover the steps and the blocked doorway. Still not knowing if this is the tomb for which he has been searching for so long, he dispatches to his patron in England a telegram that in the years to come will become world famous:

At last have made wonderful discovery in Valley; a magnificent tomb with seals intact; re-covered same for your arrival; congratulations.

It was two and a half weeks before Carnarvon reached Luxor. And for Carter's aristocratic patron, 1922 did indeed turn out to be his last digging season – just not for the reason he intended ...

They were an odd couple, Carter and Carnarvon: the driven, middle-class, self-taught Egyptologist and his debonair aristocratic patron.

Howard Carter was 48 years old in 1922. The youngest of the 11 children of a professional illustrator, he had suffered from poor health as a child and been sent from London to Norfolk to be brought up by two maiden aunts. The education he received there was limited in scope and came to an end abruptly when he reached the age of 15 and needed to start earning his living.

Fortunately for Howard Carter, he had inherited his father's talent for drawing. He soon got work as a draughtsman working for archaeologists, making meticulous copies of the carvings, paintings and writings on ancient buildings. He arrived in Egypt at the age of 17, and though he had no formal education in either ancient history or Egyptology, Carter never really went home again. He spent the rest of his professional life among the ruins of Ancient Egypt, acquiring a knowledge and reputation that was eventually to equal that of his university-educated colleagues.

It's hard to warm to Howard Carter, either from the accounts of him left by contemporaries or from the diaries he wrote. He was a difficult man, with an inferiority complex about his lack of education and a quick temper. Single-minded and meticulous about his work, he was also tactless and obstinate, with a singular ability to fall out with both fellow archaeologists and the local bureaucrats and politicians of Egypt.

His patron Lord Carnarvon was quite a different character, and a man from a very different world.

Resident at the beautiful family seat of Highclere Castle near Newbury in Berkshire, Lord Carnarvon was an aristocrat with an extensive private income. While Carter was single-mindedly devoted to Egyptology, his patron pursued with passion a wide range of pastimes and enthusiasms. He was a great gambler and not only enjoyed racing but also bred race-horses. While Carter was a batchelor, Carnarvon lived at the heart of a lively family life. In spite of being in poor health, he enjoyed flying and driving fast cars. He became fascinated by photography and had a darkroom built in the castle where he printed his own photographs. Everything about his life reveals a man of enormous energy and a very attractive spirit of engagement with life and its opportunities.

The present Lord Carnarvon describes his great-grandfather: 'He was one of the last great Edwardian adventurers ... the gentleman adventurer who went out in the world to try something new. He was really interested in new technology, new things and discovery in general ... He was a terrific character.'

When, in 1908, Lord Carnarvon was advised to spend the winter away from England – for the good of his health, weakened by a car accident – he decided to go to Egypt, and immediately immersed himself in Egyptology. He threw himself enthusiastically into amateur excavation – not very successfully. According to his great-grandson, 'At first he did it by himself, with only rather limited success I think. A vast amount of rubble and holes were dug at some expense but they found a mummified cat and not much more.'

But being Carnarvon, he was not content to leave it at that. He searched for a professional who could help him and stumbled upon Howard Carter. Carter had recently fallen out with the archaeology establishment in Egypt –

over his refusal to apologise for something that he did not consider his fault. Characteristically, a trivial misunderstanding had escalated and he had lost his comfortable job with the Antiquities Service. Carnarvon's offer of employment came at just the right time.

For 15 years these two very different men had a successful partnership in Egypt. As Carnarvon's great-grandson points out, they made a good team: the impatient explorer and venture capitalist who with his income and enthusiasm was able to back the talented, persistent but very prickly scholar.

In the early days they had much luck and some success. Carter was also able to use his position in Egypt to acquire magnificent pieces for Carnarvon's private collection. By the early 1920s it was said by some to be one of the finest private collections of Egyptian art in the world. But they both became increasingly obsessed with the search for the missing tomb of Tutankhamun. Of all the kings and queens of Ancient Egypt, Tutankhamun was one of the very few whose tomb had not been identified. It is hard to appreciate this now, when the name Tutankhamun is familiar even to primary school children, but until the early twentieth century historians knew very little about this obscure pharaoh. However, from the late 1800s, a sprinkling of clues had led Carter to believe that his tomb would be found in a certain part of the Valley of the Kings. A small faience cup with one of Tutankhamun's many names on it was found under a rock, by complete chance, by a young archaeologist named Edward Ayrton. Then, a few years later, Ayrton found a pit that contained fragments of linen and faded floral collars, the remains of a banquet and some jars. This he suspected was the debris left over from an embalming. Tutankhamun's name on some baked earth seals led Ayrton to guess the missing pharaoh was the person being embalmed. Finally, an undecorated chamber was discovered with Tutankhamun's name on some gold foil. Though the retired American lawyer and amateur archaeologist Theodore Davis, who held the 'concession' for excavating the Valley of the Kings, believed that this small chamber was Tutankhamun's tomb, Carter was unconvinced. He believed that Tutankhamun's final resting place was still to be found.

He made a careful map of the whole Valley of the Kings, marking off all the areas that had been excavated and adding to it these three new clues connected to the boy pharaoh. A small area remained unexcavated, and this was where, since 1917, Carter had been doggedly digging.

Immediately Lord Carnarvon received the momentous telegram, he made arrangements to come out to Egypt. With his daughter Evelyn, he arrived in Luxor on 23 November. The following day Carter took father and daughter to the place in the hot dry Valley of the Kings where he and his workmen had found the flight of stone steps leading down to the doorway. Work began again.

Quickly the rock and sandy earth were removed from the 13 steps. Then three more were uncovered to reveal the whole of the doorway. Though there were signs that the tomb had been broken into – probably by tomb raiders in ancient times – the hole they had made had been plugged and the replastered doorway covered with the imprint of ancient seals. As the workmen cleared away the debris towards the bottom of the door, Carter saw the name he had been longing to see: Tutankhamun. His tenacity and his hunch had paid off. This was indeed the lost tomb of the boy pharaoh.

They broke through the plastered doorway and found a passageway, sloping downwards and full of debris. There was evidence that others, intent on raiding the tomb before them, had dug a tunnel through it. Mixed with the stones were broken pottery and alabaster jars and seals. After about 10 metres of passageway they found a second doorway, blocked and again marked with official seals. There were signs that this door too had been broken into and resealed. Again, they found the cartouche of Tutankhamun. With Carnarvon, his daughter and Carter's assistant Callender gathered round, Howard Carter carefully broke a small hole in this sealed doorway and poked an iron rod into the space beyond. Then they passed a candle into the black space to check for dangerous gasses.

Every Egyptian season, Carter kept two diaries of his work. Today they are in the care of Dr Jasamir Malek at the Griffith Institute in Oxford. Together they form a fascinating record of Carter's life as an Egyptologist. The first group of diaries are small personal notebooks.

Carter wrote in them every day while he was digging, so they are an accurate on-the-spot record of his work. But most entries in these diaries simply record an unexciting list of practical details – how much the carpenter needs paying, how many workers were on the excavation team and so on. The second group of journals, it can be deduced from the handwriting, were each written all on one occasion, perhaps at the end of each season's digging, as a formal balance sheet of what he had achieved. It is from the formal diary for the 1922 season that the colourful and now world-famous descriptions of the finding of Tutankhamun's tomb are taken.

This is how Carter describes what happened next:

Widening the hole a little I inserted the candle and peered in ... At first I could see nothing, the hot air escaping causing the candle flame to flicker but presently as my eyes grew accustomed to the light, details of the room within emerged slowly from the mist. Strange animals, statues, and gold – everywhere the glint of gold. For a moment – an eternity it must have seemed to the others standing by – I was struck dumb with amazement, and when Lord Carnarvon, unable to stand the suspense any longer, inquired anxiously 'Can you see anything?' It was all I could do to get out the words, 'Yes, wonderful things.'

For by the light of the candle, and then of a torch passed

quickly forwards to him, Carter saw an extraordinary sight. A small room was crammed with an amazing range of precious objects: statues and gilded couches, beds and chariots, alabaster dishes and inlaid caskets, and two life-sized guardian statues in black and gold guarding another sealed entrance.

The quartet broke through the wall into this room, now known as the Antechamber. Then they broke through the sealed entrance between the two guardian figures and found the burial chamber of the king himself. At that moment, all they could see were the gilded panels of the outermost structure of the tomb. They would later find that there were four structures, one inside the other. And inside the innermost one lay four containers, again like Russian dolls, one inside the other. In the fourth one lay the embalmed body of Tutankhamun. Beyond the burial chamber, they later found a further storage room filled with even more precious objects.

In the whole of archaeology nothing to equal this intact tomb, crammed with treasures and the everyday objects necessary for Tutankhamun's journey into the afterlife, had ever been found.

In his diary Carter tries to capture how he felt at that extraordinary moment:

Three thousand, four thousand years maybe, have passed and gone since human feet last trod the floor on which you stand, and yet, as you note the signs of recent life around you – the half filled bowl of mortar for the door, the blackened lamp, the finger mark upon the freshly painted surface, the farewell garland dropped upon the threshold – you feel it might have been but yesterday ... Time is annihilated by little intimate details such as these and you feel an intruder.

For Dr Jasamir Malek, the intensity of emotion and the poetic tone of Carter's writing here is revealing. Carter was neither a particularly literary man, nor a poetic one. Dr Malek is convinced that the poetry of this description was the result of Carter understanding at a very deep level that he – the untrained outsider in the world of academic archaeology – had had an experience unparalleled in the whole history of Egyptian excavation. That day was a day that would never be equalled.

Untrained 'amateur' that Carter was, Malek has the highest respect for him and believes it was extremely fortunate that it fell to such a meticulous and driven man to find and excavate this treasure of Egyptology: 'I think he was a superb archaeologist, and I must say I admire him enormously because he made this wonderful discovery but was also able to record it properly in spite of all the difficulties which were put in his way. And I sometimes suspect that this was because he was a rather difficult man. Perhaps somebody who would have been more pleasant towards his collaborators, more diplomatic when it came to dealing with bureaucracy, would simply not have been able to achieve what Carter eventually did. So this, I would say, sheer bloody-mindedness eventually ensured that the discovery was properly recorded for Egyptology.'

There were five or six thousand different objects in the rooms that made up Tutankhamun's tomb. There were statues and chairs; shields and lamps and thrones; boomerangs and all kinds of boxes. There were writing materials and clothes; cups and agricultural implements; jewellery, rushwork hassocks and jars of cosmetics. Some were made of precious stones, faience, lapis lazuli, glass or gold, and of inestimable value. Others, like the collection of 130 sticks and staves, seem an odd choice for a king's tomb –though one of these, a reed stick, has a touching inscription: 'A reed which His Majesty cut with his own hand'.

Carter made sure that every one was numbered and catalogued, its original place in the tomb recorded. Every important object was sketched by Carter himself. Numerous photographs were taken. Notes were made of any inscriptions. Many of the objects – like the sandals on the floor of the Antechamber – were too fragile to be moved initially. Such objects were conserved until it was safe to move them without damage. This minutely careful recording and conserving of the contents of the tomb went on for a further 10 years and is still not published today.

But the state of euphoria that the little team of treasure seekers enjoyed on that first week of November did not last. At first they were at the centre of an exhila-

rating whirl of interest from Egyptologists, local digni-
taries, politicians, the press and members of the public.
Everything they did was greeted with excitement and
admiration. Then Carnarvon sold the rights to cover the
story of the ongoing excavation to the *Times* newspaper
and their troubles began. The international press was
frustrated and suddenly deprived of an interesting story.
The local Egyptians were infuriated, believing with some
justification that the story of Tutankhamun was naturally theirs and not Carnarvon and Carter's to control
and sell.

In an increasingly difficult atmosphere, tension
mounted between Carnarvon and Carter as well. Then,
in late February, disaster struck. Lord Carnarvon fell ill.
On 5 April he died. He was only 57.

It was with Lord Carnarvon's death that began the
enduring legend of the curse of Tutankhamun's tomb. By
coincidence, the romantic novelist Marie Correlli had just
written a newspaper article warning of the most dire
consequences for those who desecrated a pharaoh's tomb.
Her words took on the quality of a supernatural predic-
tion and within days newspapers around the world were
full of it. Stories about mysterious happenings connected
with the tomb and the team who had found it began to
circulate. Lord Carnarvon's pet terrier, Susie, dropped
dead the moment her master died in Egypt. Carter's pet
canary was said to have been eaten alive by a cobra on the
day the tomb was opened. The newspapers reported that
the lights went out all over Cairo while Carnarvon lay

dying in hospital there. A rumour was soon circulating that a secret inquiry at the highest level into this failure was unable to find any technical reason for the black-out. Then, in the months and years that followed, more and more accidents, deaths and untoward events were attributed to the curse. Lord Carnarvon's two half-brothers died prematurely, as did his secretary, and his secretary's father, Lord Westbury. At the latter's funeral a child was knocked down by the hearse and killed; an American millionaire died after visiting the tomb and catching a cold; a radiographer coming to X-ray the mummy died on his way there; an Egyptian prince was murdered shortly after visiting the tomb, while Arthur Mace, a key member of Carter's team, suffered a breakdown in health and left Egypt for good in 1924. And – most mysterious of all – when the skull of Tutankhamun was eventually unwrapped, a partly healed scar was found on his left cheek in the very same spot where the fatal mosquito had stung Lord Carnarvon ...

Most contemporary Egyptologists were swift to condemn the stories of curses and spells and supernatural happenings. But for Lord Carnarvon's own family – especially for his son, who hurried to Cairo and was only able to see his father for a few hours before he died – there was perhaps some doubt. The present Lord Carnarvon remembers his grandfather's ambivalent behaviour: 'My grandfather always used to say that it didn't mean so much to him ... But I think it did mean something to him because ... the few things he had here

… were hidden away in cupboards for 64 years. He didn't want anyone to see them or even know that they were there. So I think he was a little bit worried about his father's association with Egypt.'

But how did Egyptian mummies come to be associated with curses in the first place?

The story did not originate with Tutankhamun. It was not even a new idea in the 1920s. There were already dozens of popular novels and short stories that hinged on the idea that the ancient Egyptians had occult powers. The idea was that their mummies were able to wreak revenge on anyone who disturbed their tombs. In 1912 a mummy being transported to America in the hold of the *Titanic* was said to have caused the sinking of the ship. Sir Arthur Conan Doyle had written a popular horror story based on a vengeful mummy, as Dr Dominic Montserrat of the Open University notes: 'From the 1890s onwards we begin to see lots of stories in English fiction about vengeful mummies. And perhaps the best known is Arthur Conan Doyle's story, "Lot No. 249", of 1894, in which a man buys an Egyptian mummy at an auction, Lot No. 249, and takes it back to Oxford, where it pursues him and tries to destroy him. So we've got the idea there of the vengeful mummy who will try to get revenge on the person who has desecrated its tomb.'

But what was the origin of these fantastic stories? Were they simply traditional ghost stories with the added romantic colour of an Egyptian setting?

Many of the 'curse of Tutankhamun' stories circulating

in the 1920s take as their starting point a curse that was said to have been written in hieroglyphics over the doorway into the boy king's tomb. It was supposed to have said: 'Death shall come on swift wings to whoever toucheth the tomb of Pharaoh.' But there is no sign of any such curse over any of the doorways in the tomb, and Carter vigorously denied that there had ever been one. But stories like this die hard. The more Carter denied it, the more the story was told that, terrified by the power of the curse and wanting to deny that it was at work in the Valley of the Kings, Carter had personally had it erased from King Tut's tomb.

Dr Salima Ikram is an Egyptologist based at the American University in Cairo. She explains that curses *were* sometimes written in ancient Egyptian tombs to terrify potential tomb robbers, but very few of them threatened supernatural retribution or suggested that the mummy itself would wreak vengeance on the desecrators.

Ever since the early days of the Egyptian kingdom, around 2500 BC, tomb-raiders had been a problem. At that time the kings and nobles were buried under pyramids, with a mortuary temple beside the tomb itself. But this was tantamount to an advertisement to tomb-robbers that under the pyramid was a collection of valuable objects just waiting to be stolen. So around 1500 BC the Egyptians began to abandon pyramids altogether, building only mortuary temples where the pyramids of the past had been placed, on the very edge of the desert. Burial chambers were cut a few kilometres away in a dried up river valley now known as the Valley of the Kings.

At that time, there were tomb-robbers of every kind: poor thieves, tempted by the riches they knew were buried with the kings; nobles; and corrupt artisans who used the knowledge they had obtained as tomb-builders to become tomb-robbers. Some did not even wait for the mummy to be buried, for archaeologists have found the empty impressions made by heavy pieces of jewellery *inside* the wrappings of mummies, which could only mean that the person employed to wrap the body had at first placed the jewels there and then, a little later, had gone back, removed the expensive piece of jewellery and then gone on wrapping. Only an embalmer was in the position to do this.

In some pyramids, the passages leading to the burial chamber were closed with large stone slabs a little like portcullises, that slid up and down in grooves on either side of the passage. Archaeologists investigating many thousands of years later have sometimes found these slabs deliberately propped open on pieces of stone, so that the passage was left partially open – clear evidence that the tomb-builders intended to return later to rob the very tombs they had helped build.

There is even evidence that men employed to guard the tombs were themselves robbers.

To the man (or woman) rich enough to plan a burial in the Valley of the Kings, it was essential to defeat the tomb-robbers at all costs, for the Ancient Egyptians believed that were their mummy damaged or any of the important items removed from their tomb, they would be deprived of the afterlife. To have their tomb desecrated in this way was as bad as never having been mummified at all.

It is not surprising therefore that the Egyptians did everything to protect themselves, and their venerated ancestors and rulers, from tomb-robbers. And that protection was a very pragmatic mixture of the magical – including curses – and the highly practical.

They were, for example, in the habit of opening tombs a while after the person had been buried and secretly moving the mummy to another location to protect it. Many of the tombs also had physical barriers. They had booby traps and hidden shafts. They had dead-end false tunnels and additional walls.

They would also protect the mummy itself. Salima Ikram likens this protection to a series of Russian dolls, one inside the other. The mummy would often be inside a shrine, then inside a sarcophagus, then inside layer upon layer of wrappings. There were goddesses and genii protecting him, too, and written on the inside of the death mask were powerful spells. According to Ikram: 'There was a whole series of religious magical spells that would protect the pharaoh ... Each bandage probably had a special spell attached to it, so as they wrapped the bandages around the pharaoh, he was actually getting a cocoon of magical protection all around him. This would serve not only to help him get from this world to the next world, but also to keep away any intruders and guard his physical body from harm.'

Between the layers that swaddled his body magical amulets would also be placed to protect the pharaoh. One such amulet made of green jasper and gold and just over a centimetre long, is now at the British Museum. Once it protected the body of a king, and it should have helped to ensure his passage to the afterlife, but by an amazing series of coincidences we know that it failed in this. Curator John Taylor explains how this small magical object, carefully inscribed with hieroglyphs on its reverse, connects us directly with a tomb-raider of the time of Tutankhamun.

At that time – the twelfth century BC – tomb-robbing had become such a problem that a commission had been set up to investigate and bring to a halt the robbery of tombs in the Valley of the Kings. The British Museum holds papyrus documents that were once part of an archive specifically dealing with tomb robbery. One is the record of the inspection committee. 'They followed a path around the necropolis ... checking on all the major tombs, and as they visited each one, they made a record of what they'd discovered,' explains Dr John Taylor, Assistant Keeper of Egyptian Antiquities. 'And the hieratic text here describes each tomb that they visited. It names the king who the tomb belonged to and describes the condition of the monument. And they found that these tombs were all intact, except one. One king's tomb had been robbed.'

Another papyrus in the archive contains a record of the trial of the robbers who had robbed this particular tomb. It includes the confession of one of them. His account of breaking into the king's tomb is uncannily like Carter's account of the opening of Tutankhamun's tomb three millennia later. John Taylor is fascinated by the words of the tomb-raider that conjure up so well what went on in the darkness of the tomb that night more than 3,000 years ago: 'It's an incredibly vivid document. You actually have the words of the robber describing how he broke into the tomb, how he made his way through the underground passage with a candle in his hand and broke into the burial chamber. He found the mummy of the king lying there in its coffins, and the queen's body as well next to the king's. And he describes opening the coffins: the gold mask on the mummy's head, the gold inlays and the jewels on the coffin's surfaces. And all these were stripped off and carried away.'

The robber specifically mentions the amulets of gold that were on the neck of the king. By an extraordinary coincidence the king's name on the back of the green jasper and gold amulet that is in the Museum today shows that it was one of those very same amulets mentioned in the confession.

The papyrus gives a detailed description of the case but it does not say what happened to the thief. Tomb-robbing was considered a very serious crime meriting the most severe punishment. The story goes that archaeologists once found the remains of a man stitched into a sheep skin. As his internal organs had not been removed as would have been the case with a mummy, he was probably still alive when he was sewn into the skin. It seems likely that he was a tomb-robber, caught in the act. Tomb-robbers were often executed in public in a particularly gruesome way – by impaling on a sharpened stake.

Then there were the curses – powerful in themselves for, as Dr Ikram explains, 'The Egyptians believed that if it's written or said, it becomes the truth.'

The threats made in these curses are down to earth. '...Huge birds will come out of the sky and peck at you, crocodiles will snap you in two, hippopotami will trample you, scorpions and snakes will sting you,' says Salima Ikram. 'So it's all very much a physical thing that will occur if you dare to desecrate these tombs.'

Not all Egyptian tombs have curses and very few replicate the supernatural tone of the curse – dubbed by the *Times* 'the curse of Osiris' – that was said to have protected Tutankhamun for so long.

In spite of the booby-traps, and the occasional curse, it seems to have been much more common for tombs to be broken into and robbed than to survive intact. So why – if there was no curse operating some spectacular form of protection over Tutankhamun – did his tomb survive more than 3,000 years untouched?

It is clear from the way the doors were broken into and then replastered that two groups of robbers did in fact break in to the tomb, very early on. The first group targetted the gold and costly cosmetics left in the tomb. Carter even found footprints on the floor, and in one of the jars full of a thick and extremely valuable unguent he could see the finger marks of the robber who had scooped out the thick viscous liquid. The second group appear to have been much more organised, for they had to tunnel their way through the stone chippings that had been used to fill the tunnel between the outer and the inner doors after the first robbery. Carter estimated that a team of robbers must have worked for about eight hours to clear a way through to the burial chamber. He also estimated that they managed to steal more than half of the jewels that had originally been placed in the tomb. It seems likely they visited the tomb on a number of occasions and that at last their luck ran out. A little bundle of gold rings, wrapped in a linen scarf, was found as if it had been casually tossed back into the tomb, the man intent on stealing it having been caught red-handed. This must have taken place not long after the king's burial, and the doors would have been resealed in antiquity.

But now a scientist from outside the world of Egyptology has finally cracked the puzzle that has kept archaeologists guessing for so long. Stephen Cross is a professional meteorologist who works for the Coastguard service in Liverpool. Trained as a geologist, he has long been fascinated by the world of ancient Egypt and the mystery of why Tutankhamun's tomb remained hidden – and intact – for so long. But it was only when he visited the Griffith Institute in Oxford and saw one particular photograph that the explanation for why the tomb had remained intact hit him like a thunderbolt.

The small black and white photograph showed the entrance to the tomb – cut into the rock with a jumble of rock and earth above it. It was clearly taken soon after Carter uncovered the tomb, before the retaining wall that appears in later pictures was built. Not surprisingly, it had never been published for, to most observers, it seems without interest. But most observers are not geologists who also know about the weather. Cross thought he recognised what the photograph showed. He got out a magnifying glass and took a closer look and his first impression was confirmed: the reason why no one had found the tomb was because the entrance had been buried under debris carried down from the hills by a flash flood. 'I was absolutely stunned. It's so obviously a petrified flood layer. I thought of the hundreds of people who have seen this [photograph] before. Why hasn't anyone else come up with this flood theory? Then I realised: of course, all the people who would look at this before would be Egyptologists. You couldn't expect an Egyptologist who hasn't a geologist's training to recognise a flood layer on sight.'

Flash floods are relatively common in this part of Egypt. About every ten years or so enormous thunder clouds gather in autumn and drop their rain. 'One cloud can hold up to half a million tonnes of water, and because of the life cycle of a cloud it drops within about 20 minutes. All that water dropping vertically on to the Valley is an absolute catastrophe.'

The Valley of the Kings is like an amphitheatre with high cliffs and steep-sided narrow valleys. In a flash flood, enormous quantities of rain water rush down these steep slopes, scouring away soil and tearing up rocks. This powerful flood is funnelled down to the bottom of the valley, where the water leaves its load of earth, rocks and gravel.

Steve Cross knew about flash floods and the Valley of the Kings. He knew that some ancient Egyptian tombs had been badly damaged by flooding. But it was only when he began to look in detail at the geological map – in relation to Tutankhamun's tomb – that he realised quite why the tomb had been so effectively hidden. As many as three different streams – each with a load of flood debris – would have converged on it and deposited there. The size of the boulders in the layer of flood debris visible on the photograph – one is clearly 60cm across – indicates that this flood was exceptionally powerful. As the rain passed, the hot Egyptian sun would have come out and baked the new layer of mud and rock until it was as hard as concrete. To a passer-by, the 1 metre thick layer of flood debris on top of the tomb would now look just like the valley floor. No wonder it took the archaeologists so long to find it.

Steve thinks he has also solved the mystery of why the tomb was not more extensively plundered in ancient times. Examining the photograph in detail he could see that there was no material at all between the rock and the flood layer. Not even windblown sand. It therefore seems likely to him that this flash flood happened very soon after Tutankhamun's burial. 'We know from the flowers found in Tutankhamun's tomb, that he was buried about March–April of the year that he died. And the floods usually happen October to November at the start of Autumn. I speculate the tomb was only open to view for six or seven months of the year that Tutankhamun died.'

It seems likely therefore that the two robberies happened in the first months after he was buried. Steve suspects these robbers would have been the very workmen from the nearby village of Deir el Medina who would have cut the tomb in the first place. But once the flood came down, not even these locals – who knew the Valley better than anyone else – would have been able to find the tomb and its fabulous treasures again. 'After the flood, not only was the tomb entrance concealed, but it was covered by what was effectively three feet of rein-forced concrete. It would have been very difficult indeed to try and hack through that and get to the tomb entrance.'

After that, the tomb remained intact until 1922. Chance seems to have intervened on Tutankhamun's side. His was a very small and unimpressive tomb for a pharaoh, and within a short time it was half buried by Ramesses VI's much more impressive one, which was built on top of it and so covered it up. There were also so few references to Tutankhamun's life and career on the monuments of his time that historians knew very little about him before his tomb was found.

Crucial to a better understanding of his story was the embalmed body that Carter and his team found concealed within its protective nests of gilded panelling and coffins. In 1925 an autopsy was begun on the mummy by Douglas Derry, Professor of Anatomy at the Egyptian University of Cairo.

With a brutality and clumsiness that astonishes present day forensic archaeologists, Derry and his team undertook an extensive and highly invasive series of operations on the body. The limbs were all removed and several of them were broken in more than one place. The skull was detached from the body and the body itself was even sawn in half.

From this investigation Derry was able to establish some basic facts about the young king. From the development of his bones and teeth, he estimated that Tutankhamun was around 18 years old when he died. He was a slightly built young man, about 1m 65cm tall.

But nothing in the examination of his body enabled Derry to determine how or why the young pharaoh met his death.

In 1968, another investigation was made into the body of the dead king. Professor R G Harrison led a team from Liverpool University to Luxor. In extremely difficult conditions – as Robert Connolly, who was involved in pioneering blood-typing work on the mummy, recalls – a mobile hand-held X-ray machine was taken into Tutankhamun's tomb and used to X-ray the body. Not knowing what was inside the skull, the team did not know how long to expose it for. Nor could they manage to get the skull completely straight. They then made a dark room in the bathroom of the local hotel and printed the plates.

The resulting X-rays of Tutankhamun's skull have been pored over and studied for more than 30 years. And the more they have been studied, the more the mysteries and the stories grow about the pharaoh and a powerful curse. But this time the curse afflicts not those who disturb the pharaoh's rest but the king himself. For the story goes that the young king was murdered.

Dr Aidan Dodson is an Egyptologist from Bristol University. He lists the reasons why investigators have thought Tutankhamun's skull raises suspicions: 'Tutankhamun's death around the age of 18 has always been something of a mystery. All sorts of theories have been put about. X-rays of the skull of his mummy suggest that there may have been some kind of cerebral haemorrhage around the time of death. There's also an injury on the side of his face just in front of the ear ... There's the fact that the skull of the mummy has been shaved, which is very, very unusual for the preparation of mummies, so there is some indication his death may have been the result of some kind of head injury. But what caused the head injury is anybody's guess.'

Researchers have also commented on the fact that the

skull is unnaturally thin and that a small fragment of bone appears inside the skull on the X-ray, as does a curious line. All these clues have been interpreted to suggest that the young king died from a blow to the head.

But Robert Connolly disagrees. The line – which some have thought to be a calcified membrane, the result of severe bruising or a cerebral haemorrhage to the back of the head – is in fact in his opinion nothing more sinister than the other side of the head appearing on the X-ray, a function of the fact that Harrison's team were unable to get the head straight when they X-rayed it. The thinning of the skull is within the range of what is normal. The partly healed lesion on the cheek could have been the result of nothing more sinister than a mosquito bite. The fragment of bone lodged inside the skull that some have thought was caused by a blow to the head, Connolly is convinced – judging by the lack of any obvious damage to the skull, and the bone's shape – is a piece of neck bone, forced into the skull by the clumsy efforts of Derry's autopsy. He commented: 'Murder is unlikely, or at least there's no evidence from the skeleton for murder.'

But Connolly, who has studied the X-rays in some detail, believes they do suggest a possible cause of death. The sternum is missing from the skeleton, as is the collar bone and some of the ribs. And this is not the first time injuries of this kind have been found on a skeleton. Some time ago a medieval skeleton was disinterred in Cumbria. The man was known to have died in a jousting accident and his injuries were very similar to those of the young Tutankhamun. There is much evidence that Tutankhamun was a keen huntsman, for his tomb was packed with bows and boomerangs and other hunting weapons. On the walls of the tomb and on one of the many decorated boxes are pictures of him hunting. Perhaps he died in a hunting accident or was kicked in the chest by his horse. Perhaps he fell from his own chariot and died from crushing injuries.

For Connolly, however, though the evidence is consistent with such an accidental death, the explanation for the damage to the boy king's chest is ultimately altogether more prosaic and less illuminating. He thinks it was actually caused by Dr Derry when he undertook the autopsy in the 1920s, as he tried to chisel the magnificent gold death mask from the mummy. Says Connolly: 'What everybody always wants to know every time we have a body is what was the cause of death. I'm afraid we still now have to say we don't know.'

However all kinds of other archaeological clues suggest that Tutankhamun's death was sudden and unexpected and so may well have been the result of an accident rather than an illness. The tomb itself is very small and unimpressive for a pharaoh. It seems likely that Tutankhamun had not yet begun to think about preparing for his death. When he did die, his entourage were forced to bury him in a tomb that had been built for someone else, perhaps his military leader, General Ay. There is plenty of evidence, too, that the whole procedure was rushed. The embalming was done rather badly. A small gilded mask that had been made for one of the two mummified foetuses found in the tomb which Connolly was able to establish, by blood typing, were most likely Tutankhamun's stillborn children clearly did not fit when it came to the moment, and so it was dumped, along with the detritus from the funeral feast. Inside the canopic chest that held some of the internal organs of the pharaoh, are carved heads that do not really look like the king and beautifully carved gold coffins that have had the names on the cartouches altered from the original. The photographs Carter and Carnarvon took also suggest that the filling and sealing of the tomb was done in something of a hurry, with the mass of objects finally crammed in any old how.

Careful examination of the thousands of objects in the tomb and the many detailed pictures and wall paintings have helped historians piece together a fuller picture of the young pharaoh, his interests, his religious beliefs, his tastes and his personal history. Tutankhamun was the only surviving son of Akhenaten, the famous 'heretical' pharaoh who tried to abolish thousands of years of Egyptian religion in favour of a single sun god. It seems Tutankhamun was only around eight years old when he succeeded his father on the throne. As was the custom, he married his elder sister and they became together the king and queen of Egypt. The land he inherited was very wealthy. As one of his contemporaries is believed to have said, 'There is more gold in Egypt than sand; and there's a lot of sand.'

Within a few years Tutankhamun began to restore the old gods. Three men – all from the military – ruled in his name when he was a boy, and it seems likely that it was they who wanted a return to the old religious ways. There is evidence, too, that this may have been popular, for even under Akhenaten the ordinary people continued worshipping the old gods.

Then, when he was barely 18, Tutankhamun died suddenly. Aidan Dodson picks up the story of what happened next: 'On Tutankhamun's death, his wife did a very strange thing for an Egyptian queen. She wrote to the king of the Hittites … (basically modern Turkey) and said, "My husband is dead, I have no son. Will you send one (of your sons) to me? I will marry him and make him king of Egypt." The Hittite King was incredulous at this. "Never before has this happened," he says in a later inscription. So he sent an envoy to Egypt to find out if this was actually true. He came back and said, yes, it was indeed true; the king was dead and there was no heir.'

So a Hittite prince was dispatched to Egypt to marry Tutankhamun's widow and become Pharaoh. But he never arrived. Somewhere in Palestine he was set upon and murdered.

Aidan Dodson has examined the paintings on the walls of Tutankhamun's tomb in great detail. In the light of this story, he makes sense of the paintings that show Ay, who succeeded Tutankhamun to the throne and was possibly Tutankhamun's father-in-law, making the final offerings to the dead: 'According to Egyptian law, if you carried out the burial of somebody as if you were their son, you were the legitimate heir to their possessions and so on. And that is the only time we ever see one king burying a previous king actually on the wall of a tomb. It's clearly in the wake of the problems caused by the queen attempting to bring a Hittite onto the throne. This is probably the reason why Ay felt it necessary to make sure that he was doing things properly in front of the gods.'

However, Ay's reign did not last long either. He was succeeded by Horemheb, who was a younger man. It is thanks to Horemheb that Tutankhamun's name was once so little known, for all over Egypt, he set about erasing it, chiselling flat the oval cartouches in which it had been written on public monuments and substituting his own name instead. It was only when Edward Ayrton stumbled on the evidence 3,000 years later that Egyptologists like Carter began to be obsessed with the idea of finding his tomb.

The story of a vengeful mummy attacking the archaeologists who had finally disturbed its rest may be hard to believe. But recently evidence has been coming to light that suggests archaeologists may actually run quite a risk when they investigate the tombs of the pharaohs.

Dr Gavin Gillmore of Bradford University has been looking at the dangers posed to guides and archaeologists working in the tombs of the Middle East by a gas called radon. He says, radon is 'colourless, odourless and tasteless, so you can't see it. You donknow it's there.'

Radon is a product of the breaking down of uranium, which is a chemical very commonly found in rocks. The gas itself is not radioactive but once it is in the lungs it starts to do damage. The breakdown products of the gas remain in fragile lung tissue and do harm after the gas itself has been exhaled. Lung cancer, prostate cancer, skin cancer and cancer of the red bone marrow have all been linked with exposure to radon. The longer the exposure the greater the risk. It is now thought that in the United Kingdom around 2,000 people a year die as a result of contact with radon. The National Radiological Protection Board sets safe levels for the UK. 200 becquerels per cubic metre is considered the upper limit for a home. 400 becquerels per cubic metre is the limit at which remedial measures should be undertaken in the workplace.

But radon has qualities that means it presents a particular hazard in underground tombs like those of Tutankhamun. Says Gillmore: 'It's also very dense, so it'll tend to collect in caves, mines and homes, and particularly in something like a tomb, which is in a sense a man-made cave.'

Tombs have been tested in Jordan and levels of more than 5,000 becquerels per cubic metre have been found. Experts have estimated that the level would have been around 1,000 becquerels per cubic metre in Tutankhamun's tomb after it had been opened and air had been able to circulate. At the moment Carter broke open the sealed door and the air that had been trapped inside for 3,000 years rushed out, the levels could have been much higher.

Dr Gillmore's research suggests archaeologists working in underground caves are especially at risk. Because they are doing hard physical work they are breathing hard and drawing radon and dust deep into their lungs.

And there's another invisible danger lurking in these tombs: mould spores. Spores are the reproductive part of fungi. They are in the air around us all the time, and most of the different kinds of spores, most of the time, don't cause any problems. But there are some mould spores that are highly dangerous.

Dr David Denning, consultant in infectious diseases at Wythenshawe Hospital in Manchester, undertakes research into mould spores. It's important work because recent research into the cause of death of patients at a teaching hospital found that 1 in 25 of those who died had an invasive fungal infection due to mould spores. He says: 'In a typical room you may breathe in 30 spores in an hour … Large densities of spores are found in certain environments such as cellars. In a dusty cellar or in a hay barn, which is another very high-spore environment, you may breathe in a million spores in a minute.'

These spores are especially dangerous for people with allergies, asthma and other respiratory problems. Frequently the spores simply aggravate those breathing problems but in cases where mould spores invade the tissue of the lungs, the results can be fatal. About half of those whose lungs become 'invaded' in this way are dead within a month.

The tomb of an Egyptian mummy can prove the ideal environment for mould spores to flourish: 'There's food and it's damp and it's warm and it's just a perfect place to live for these fungi,' explains Dr Denning. 'Mould will grow on any warm environment with a lot of food – leather or plant material. In fact, many of these fungi are found in large quantities in compost heaps, so over the many thousands of years in a tomb, when the food degrades naturally, you'd expect to find a large amount of fungal spores there.'

So were radon and mould spores responsible for the deaths of those who desecrated Tutankhamun's tomb?

If high concentrations of radon gas and mould spores were in Tutankhamun's tomb, then Lord Carnarvon could have been affected by them both. However, in the 1920s little was known about either hazard. His death certificate notes that he died of pneumonia, which had developed, along with a severe infection, following a mosquito bite on his cheek. But it is perfectly possible that the culprit was in fact a mould spore that he had inhaled while working in the tomb. No one will ever know.

But what of his companions in the Valley of the Kings?

A famous photograph shows Carter and his team dining in the tomb during the excavations. These were the men who were most at risk from radon and from mould spores – as well as, presumably, from any supernatural powers. Yet it seems they avoided all these dangers, living to an average of 66 years old. Carter himself lived on for another 17 years after finding the tomb – many of which he spent labouring in the close confines of the tomb itself. He was 65 when he died. Lord Carnarvon's daughter, Lady Evelyn, did not die until 1979.

Of those many people whose deaths have been attributed to the curse over the years, most had not come anywhere near the tomb.

A further mystery surrounds why the story of the curse arose in first place and why it took such a hold on people's imagination.

Dr Dominic Montserrat of the Open University suggests that the idea of a curse attached to this particular mummy's tomb served a useful purpose for the large team of archaeologists working over many years to excavate its fabulous treasures: 'It's ... possible that the whole idea of the curse was encouraged by the excavators, who of course were faced with a terrific security problem in the Valley of the Kings. And the idea of a vengeful mummy was really quite a good deterrent against thieves.'

If they did indeed initiate the idea of there being something dangerous about the tomb – or at least let the rumour run – the archaeologists, as Dominic Montserrat points out, were merely reflecting the world Tutankhamun had himself come from: 'In some ways, it's going back to ancient Egyptian ideas of creating a sort of zone of fear around the dead to keep away marauders.'

But the archaeologists doggedly and meticulously

clearing the tomb were not the only ones who could have had an interest in encouraging the story of the curse. The discovery of the tomb had been a media sensation when it first hit the press in December 1922. 'Tutmania' swept Britain. The management of the *Times* newspaper who had paid Lord Carnarvon for the exclusive on the dig must have been pretty satisfied with the deal. But by the spring of 1923 excitement had waned.

'By March, people were getting pretty tired of it and you actually find them writing letters to the papers saying, "We want to read about the Tariff Act rather than about Tutenkhamun. We're really, really bored with this." I think that sheds quite an interesting light on the whole development of the curse story, because creating a curse around Tutenkhamun's death gave a really interesting new spin on the story which might enable journalists to keep covering it.'

Arthur Weigall, who succeeded Carter as Inspector General of Antiquities in Luxor – and was his rival in archaeology – became special correspondent for the *Daily Mail*, a competitor of the *Times*. While Carter was publicly condemning those naïve people who blamed Carnarvon's death on a curse, Weigall was quite happy to play along, using his position as a respected archaeologist to publish stories of his life in Egypt that encouraged a belief in the mysterious.

But whatever the motives of those who first began to spread the story, why did such a fanciful tale prove so popular and so enduring?

The idea that archaeologists, who treated the bones and the possessions of the dead simply as curiosities, were violating some deep taboo and therefore running some indefinable but serious risk, ran deep in the general population. It made sense to people that the breaking of this taboo might unleash forces both uncontrollable and unknown. It was logical to them that Carnarvon, who had not only financed the excavation and been present at the moment of the opening of the tomb, but who also appeared to be profiting from the discovery should have been the first to die.

Carnarvon himself moved in a world where the occult and the supernatural were given a high profile. Among his varied hobbies and passions Carnarvon numbered – like many in his aristocratic circle – spiritualism and palmistry. In the wake of his death, all manner of occultists rushed to make the manner of his passing appear as supernatural and sinister as possible.

He was closely linked with a palmist known as 'the Seer Velma'. Velma claimed that he had twice predicted Carnarvon's death while reading the aristocrat's palm. On the second occasion both he and Carnarvon had looked into a crystal ball and seen not just an ancient Egyptian funeral but also Carnarvon himself digging at a tomb around which powerful occult forces swirled.

A well-known clairvoyant, an Irishman known professionally as 'Cheiro', also wrote that he had had a warning – this time directly from an ancient Egyptian princess. He claimed to have written to Carnarvon to advise him not to return to Egypt.

Sir Arthur Conan Doyle, creator of Sherlock Holmes, was perhaps the most famous contemporary enthusiast for all things supernatural. When Carnarvon's sudden death was announced, Conan Doyle told the newspapers that nothing was more likely than that his death had been caused by occult forces, called 'elementals', which could have been lingering in the tomb. When he was asked why other members of the team had not also been struck by the curse, Conan Doyle had the perfect response: 'It is nonsense to say that because "elementals" do not harm everybody, therefore they do not exist. One might as well say that because bulldogs do not bite everybody, therefore bulldogs do not exist.'

Even those who might previously have scoffed at the idea of the dead exerting an influence beyond the grave were willing to entertain the notion in the emotionally charged atmosphere of Britain in the 1920s. When Carter uncovered the tomb, the First World War had been over for a little under four years. Millions of people had lost husbands, fathers and sons in the war. Millions more had been bereaved by the deadly Spanish flu that killed with astonishing, incomprehensible swiftness in 1918 and seemed to pick especially the young.

In this context, all kinds of alternative forms of spirituality had become very popular. Astrology, palmistry and especially spiritualism swept the country. People who might once have dismissed seances as nonsense, eagerly tried to get in touch with their dead loved ones.

Supernatural explanations of mysterious goings-on suddenly seemed perfectly plausible. The story of the Angel of Mons, for instance, in which an angel was said to have appeared to retreating British soldiers in August 1914, spread with equal speed.

It was not just a time of great loss of life. There was a revolution in Russia. There had been rebellion in Ireland and now the island was divided. In Britain, the Labour Party had come to power for the first time. Women had the vote. Many were now working and financially independent and were wearing shorter skirts and even smoking. It was a time, Dr Montserrat suggests, of profound uncertainty when people were ready to turn to alternative religion and were also keen to look back to see what ancient cultures could offer.

It was into this social maelstrom, that the story of the curse of Tutankhamun's vengeful mummy was released. Its popularity and longevity owe little to the culture and spiritual powers of Tutankhamun's time. It owes everything to the anxieties and doubts of the particular time when his glorious tomb, with its fabulous treasures, was uncovered and revealed to an astounded and admiring world.

CHAPTER 3

The Mystery of the Nasca Lines

In the 1920s when people first flew across southern Peru they made an astonishing discovery. Stretching below them written in the earth of this remote desert region were thousands of gigantic drawings: animals, insects and birds; long, long straight lines and odd geometric shapes.

How long had the drawings been there, unremarked, in this remote desert? Who could have drawn such gigantic pictures? How were they able to draw, with such precision, images that can only really be appreciated from the sky? And – the most intriguing question of all – why on earth did they do it?

This is the story of the mystery of those desert drawings, which have come to be known as the Nasca Lines.

In the far south-western corner of Peru, 400 kilometres from the capital, Lima, is a high plateau called the

Nasca pampa. Bounded by a narrow fertile strip that hugs the Pacific coast on one side, and by the towering snowcapped Andes on the other, this is one of the most desolate landscapes on earth.

From the air, the land is beige and brown, scarred and crumpled, cut through by deep river gorges and riven by a mass of dried-up stream beds. It is arid and forbidding from a distance and on the ground it is dusty, hot and monotonous. There is no vegetation of any kind here. No birds call. No insects buzz. The silence is absolute. It is rarely windy and there aren't even any clouds in the sky to vary the light and cause a shadow to move across the land. On the rare occasions when people are walking on the pampa, they can clearly hear each other call from half a kilometre away.

It almost never rains on the pampa; the official tally is 0.5 mm of rain per year. And the air is so dry that the mark of raindrops of a shower that fell briefly four years ago are still there, marking the dust on rocks with strangely tragic splashes.

Yet this remote and almost unpopulated desert holds some secret. For a person walking across this bare and dusty land would find – scattered as if carelessly across the sterile wasteland – the most unexpected and extraordinary evidence of some ancient and vanished civilisation. There are shards of chunky pottery, decorated in bright colours with stylised images of birds and mythical creatures. There are ruined buildings, some made of stone, others made of adobe and almost indistinguishable now from the reddish brown of the desert earth itself. There are strange small mounds – surely man-made – and stone cairns. Most extraordinary of all, there are skeletons – bleached a snowy white by the sun, curled in a foetal position and wrapped in pieces of dun-coloured woven cloth, their skulls gleaming in the bright sunlight.

Who were these people? When did they live on the Nasca plateau? And how did they survive to build a life in such a dry and barren land?

And there is something stranger still about this desert land, a mystery that can only really be appreciated from the air and that only emerged in the late 1920s when planes first began to fly across this remote region of Peru. Looking down from their cockpits, these early twentieth-century pilots had for the first time a bird's eye view of this desert. And what they saw was astonishing. Spread across the desert, over an area around 500 square kilometres, were thousands of enormous line drawings.

Some are in the shape of living things: birds, monkeys, lizards and a whale. There are plants and fishes too. Some of the images, like the humming birds, for instance, are realistic and easily identified. Others can be identified as local South American species but they have been drawn with baffling mistakes, or deliberate inaccuracies. The monkey, with its front paws pointing inwards and arched back, for instance, has a great curling tail like the South American spider monkey, but the tail curls the other way from that of a real monkey. Other drawings are highly stylised – like the carob tree with its symmetrical pattern of roots and branches (or is it seaweed?); or the magnificent bird figure, with its elongated zigzag neck that immediately conjures up the sight of a sleek black cormorant dropping like a stone towards the sea. Some figures are imaginary composite creatures, part bird, part insect, and defy definition.

But, as you fly over this barren landscape, the commonest 'Lines' to be seen are the geometric shapes. There are spirals and zigzags. There are the blunt triangles that the experts called trapezoids. And there are long, long straight lines, some leading like the spokes of a wheel back to some central point, usually a small mound; others simply heading out across the land, disappearing into the shimmering distance.

Most of the drawings are enormous: the humming bird is 90 metres long. The condor has a wing span of 137 metres and the largest of the trapezoids covers 100,000 square metres. And two generations after the aviators who first saw the Nasca Lines, it was discovered that the long straight lines – the longest of which stretches unbroken for 65 kilometres – can even be seen from space.

Overlapping and criss-crossing as they do, it's impossible to be sure exactly how many Lines there are. One small area of plateau has over 900. But one local pilot, who has been overflying the Lines and photographing them for more than 40 years, estimates that the total number is more than 3,000.

In the 1930s, as aerial photographers, archaeologists, journalists and travellers descended on Nasca to see the Lines for themselves and seek to unravel their mysterious origins, the first question they asked was, how did the line builders make them in the first place?

From the air, the making of these geoglyphs seems an extraordinary undertaking. But down on the desert floor the technique turns out to be less of a mystery. To make a Nasca Line is in fact quite simple. The surface of the pampa is covered with a coarse layer of rocks, stone and gravel called desert pavement, the remains of rocks carried down from the Andes by floods hundreds of thousands of years ago. Over the centuries the surface of this desert pavement has been darkened by exposure to the air, so the ground is naturally a dark grey-brown. But remove these darker rocks with their patina of time, and a tremendous contrast is revealed: the sand beneath is much lighter-coloured, more of a cream than a brown. The Line builders simply had to remove one layer of rock systematically to make their great pale-coloured pictures. It would not have required any tools more sophisticated than baskets to transport the stones.

But what is so impressive about the Lines is not the fact that someone worked out that by removing a layer of stones from the desert, big pictures could be made. After all, figures like England's Uffington White Horse were made many centuries ago by removing turf from a shape to reveal the gleaming white chalk beneath. What impressed explorers to Nasca was the fact that the drawings appear to be so symmetrical and perfectly made, in spite of being both so large and sometimes so complicated. Surely, people reasoned, it would have been impossible for the Line builders to achieve such precision unless (like present-day visitors) they were able to see their handiwork from the air.

People were also bemused as to why anyone would go to the immense trouble of building these gigantic pictures when they can only really be seen from the air.

In the late 1960s, Swiss author Erich von Daniken came to Nasca and declared that he had the answer. Looking down at the long, blunted triangles, the trapezoids, from a small plane, he saw only one purpose and one explanation: they had been built as landing strips for spacecraft. And the Line builders must have been aliens. His book *Chariots of the Gods* became an international sensation, selling more than 7 million copies, and the alien landing strip solution to the mystery of the Nasca Lines became much more popular and well-known than the ideas circulating at the same time amongst archaeologists and historians. For many people there was something very appealing about von Daniken's explanation. It solved the mystery of how such gigantic and precise drawings could have been made: they must somehow have involved a people who could fly. It also solved the mystery of how things that were so complicated and skilful could have been built in ancient times.

To science fiction enthusiasts, two other pieces of evidence seemed to lend support to von Daniken's extra terrestrial theory.

Among the pictures of animals and birds at Nasca there was one very strange shape – a figure not quite human, with an elongated body and huge owlish eyes, gazing forwards, one arm raised. It seems crudely drawn compared to many of the other pictures and its legs end in the odd boot shaped feet that children draw. Some Nasca researchers have expressed doubts about the authenticity of this figure, which was only 'discovered' in the 1980s. To von Daniken enthusiasts, the figure is an astronaut, beckoning to his comrades to come down to earth.

Then, archaeologists excavating the ancient ruins on the pampa made an extraordinary find. Among the skeletons found at one ancient burial site were skulls of a simply astonishing shape. Apparently human at the front, they sweep back twice the length of a normal human skull and taper to a point. Here was the classic image of the pointy-headed alien. So striking are these skulls to anyone who sees them that – in spite of the fact they are on public display in a local museum – feverish conspiracy claims shuttle back and forth on the Web claiming that governments have tried to prevent photographs of them being published.

Archaeologists have a different explanation for who built the Lines.

Dr Markus Reindel is an archaeologist from the German Archaeological Institute in Bonn. For 20 years he has been excavating ancient settlements all around the pampa, trying to piece together a picture of the civilisation that flourished here more than 1,500 years ago, a people archaeologists call the Nascans. The people archaeologists are sure were the Line builders.

Today Reindel is excavating the Nascan settlement of Los Molinos. It is in a narrow ravine that opens into one of the deep river valleys that cut through the pampa. The sides of the river valley are bare rock but the valley floor itself, watered for those four months of the year when the river runs, fed by melting snow from the high Andes, is a densely cultivated emerald strip of vegetation in the grey and white landscape.

The Nascans did not write, and their civilisation had disappeared nearly a thousand years before the Spanish reached this part of South America, so archaeologists like Reindel must use a mixture of science, anthropology and imaginative guesswork to understand their world.

Though the Nascans lived in a landscape that seems to us almost unbelievably harsh, their culture and society was far from primitive. From the evidence of their houses, Reindel has discovered that Los Molinos, at least, was a large and flourishing community. He has found huge buildings with adobe walls and numerous rooms opening off corridors and terraces.

Alongside the large residences were smaller, poorer homes. Here would have lived a community of farmers, administrators, workmen, craftsmen and priests.

From the evidence of the houses and of the many graves he has excavated, Reindel has found that this was a complex, stratified society. Some graves are of poorer people; others are of quite a different class. They contain beautiful pottery, decorated with colourful designs of animals, people and gods. The archaeologists have also found traces of gold, from rich jewellery long since stolen by grave robbers. Among the mummified bodies they have found people with elaborate hairstyles – people who had time and leisure to care for and cultivate their appearance.

Day after day, Reindel and his team patiently sift through the earth that is dug from the excavation site, passing it through sieves. It is from the smallest fragments of evidence that details about the Nascans and their way of life emerges. Broken bones, pieces of seashell, strips of cloth – all tell a story that, detective-like, Reindel can decipher. The textiles are woven from alpaca wool and among the animal bones are those of llamas. There are fish bones and remains of shellfish from the coast, and there are also spondylus shells – a rare shellfish found only in present day Ecuador, more than 2,000 kilometres north of Nasca. All these pieces of evidence tell Reindel that the people of Los Molinos must have had trading connections and would themselves have travelled many hundreds and even thousands of kilometres up and down the coast of South America and up into the Andes.

The first recognisably Nascan culture emerged around 40 BC. Tracing the development of pottery and textiles, experts have established six different phases of Nascan culture that they call, somewhat prosaically, Nasca 1 to 6. Each phase has a distinctive pottery style, a style mirrored in the woven textiles that – preserved by the desiccated desert air – still retain some of the vibrancy of their original colours. Then, some time in the sixth century AD, it seems from the archaeological evidence that the Nascan culture disappeared.

Los Molinos is not the only Nascan site to have been carefully excavated. At a place called Cahuachi, Italian archaeologist Giuseppe Orefici has uncovered a Nascan ceremonial centre spread over hundreds of acres. At its heart is a stepped pyramid, 30 metres high, and around it 40 other structures. There is no evidence here of craftsmen or farmers. It seems that the only people who lived at Cahuachi were priests. From the skeletons, forensic anthropologists have established that the Nascans at Cahuachi were relatively healthy, with strong teeth and an average life expectancy of around 37. The skeletons showed no evidence at all of the kinds of marks left on bones by fighting and war. And nearly all – more than 90 per cent – had the extraordinary elongated skulls that some people like to think are of Alien origin.

In fact the deliberate deforming of the human skull is a practice that was common in the past, and not just in South America. Such elongated skulls have been found all over central Asia, where the practice was common among nomadic tribes, such as the Huns, who swept into the Roman empire in the third and fourth centuries. They seem to have brought the custom with them, for deformed skulls have been found in Dark Age cemeteries as far west as France. It's possible the people of western Europe were so impressed by the military prowess and culture of the Huns that they wanted their children to look like them. And it is easy when a baby is young and the skull is soft to force it to grow in a particular shape. The skull simply needs to be bound tight with cloth or leather, or crushed against a wooden board. Archaeologists believe the Nascans may have deformed their skulls in this way to try to look like the gods.

Over the centuries Cahuachi has been systematically robbed by treasure seekers but there still remain numerous fascinating graves that provide another glimpse into the Nascan mind. Here are the skulls of people who met violent deaths. Ritual sacrifices perhaps. Certainly ritual burials. One skull has its mouth pinned shut with a cactus thorn. Others have their tongues cut out. Others are drilled with holes so they can be carried around, strung on a thread, perhaps as some kind of trophy.

But can we be sure it was the Nascans who built the Lines? And when did they do it?

Markus Reindel is a circumspect scientist. He proceeds with infinite care, amassing evidence and making modest statements. He has no time for the many fanciful theories that have been suggested for how and why the Lines were built. And in his opinion there's one good reason why there have been so many theories and why they have been able to flourish, even the most fanciful. No one has ever properly mapped and catalogued all the Lines, so everyone has been able to take those Lines that fit their own pet theory and ignore the rest. Until there is a proper map of all the Lines this will go on. Some lines are not easy to see. Others have been damaged. Even today, careless tourists in jeeps or farmers eager to extend land under cultivation thoughtlessly destroy Lines.

So Reindel has been carefully mapping the different Lines, trying to draw up a definitive catalogue. He sees a slow evolution over time. The Lines were not all built at the same time but developed over a thousand years. The figures came first. Reindel has found figures that date back to 800 BC. These early drawings were done on rock, not on the desert itself, and they were small.

Then the Nascans began to make the straight lines. Many of these intersect or cross over the figures, showing that they were made later. Last of all came the geometric wedges, the trapezoids. During the last years of Nascan civilisation – before it vanished completely in the sixth century AD – Reindel has discovered that buildings were constructed over earlier

Lines, as if the people no longer respected, or trusted, the giant markings in the desert.

Through studying the Lines and their interconnection, it is possible to establish an evolution but it is not possible to date the Lines themselves. Carbon dating needs some kind of organic material: rock and sand do not reveal their age. But the builders of the Lines have inadvertantly left clues for the archaeologists to unravel. Scattered on many of the Lines are shards of pottery that can be matched to the different pottery styles associated with the different phases of Nascan culture. These can be used to date the drawings. But this is not absolute proof, for the pieces of pottery could have landed on the Lines by chance at a different time, or have been dropped there by tomb raiders from another era.

So in the year 2000, Markus Reindel began to investigate the small stone mounds that are built close to many of the Lines. When he dug into these mounds he found pottery, but he also found fruit and spondylus shells. By carbon dating the fruit and cross-matching the evidence of the ceramics with ceramics found in distinct archaeological layers that he has been able to date by traditional stratigraphic methods, he has been able to confirm his theory about the broad evolution of the Lines.

As well as dating the Lines, Reindel and his team are measuring and recording them, gradually building up the first comprehensive and accurate catalogue to date. And the more Lines he maps, the more Reindel has become convinced that many of the cherished theories about the Nasca lines are simply untrue.

Firstly, their uniqueness. 'The Lines are not actually unique to Nasca,' he explains. 'It's just the best place to make them – the easiest and the place where they have survived.'

Up on the pampa, he argues, the flat land is like a gigantic blackboard, simply waiting to be drawn upon. And the combination of dark stones and pale undersoil made it easy for the drawings to be created here. Finally, the dry conditions, the lack of wind at ground level and the isolation of the area mean that they have survived for over 1,500 years.

Aurelio Rodriguez is a Peruvian archaeologist at the Catholic University of Lima. He has been looking for Lines similar to the famous ones at Nasca and what he has found supports Reindel's theory. He has discovered that there are geoglyphs up and down the Peruvian coast and the coast of Chile too. In the area around Lima alone, he has found 20 new sites where there are geoglyphs.

Like Reindel he is determined to make a definitive map. But he is in a race against time. Whereas Nasca is remote, urban growth around Lima is destroying the evidence day by day. Even a footprint is enough to damage these thousand-year-old drawings. So Aurelio uses low-tech methods to catalogue them before it is too late. He ties cameras to remote-controlled aeroplanes and small gas-filled balloons and flies them over the Lines taking photographs.

Reindel's second discovery is enough to dismay those who attribute an almost mystical quality to the Lines – an accuracy that suggests their builders had exceptional mathematical knowledge and skill: 'One thing that our mapping showed is that it is not even true that the lines are always accurate and straight. In many cases, they are slightly curved, and so they are not so accurate as people think.'

Finally, he subverts the assumption that making the Lines and pictures was an undertaking so difficult that the Line-makers must have had superhuman strength and numbers as well as hot air balloons (or space ships) to enable them to see their pictures from the air: 'You don't need complicated techniques to make a straight line. Just put down a rod and tell people to follow it to another rod and you are designing a straight line ... It's not difficult. Still today, people are making straight lines to make fields.'

In one remote place – 16 or 18 kilometres out into the pampa – American researcher David Johnston recently found just these tools. By a half finished trapezoid shape he found a bundle of stakes and baskets with stones still in them – all that was necessary to make the shape. Yet, for some reason, 1,500, 2,000 years ago the builders of that particular Line had stopped, put their materials down and never picked them up again. No one will ever know why.

Reindel is not the only one to cast doubt on the superhuman skills of the Line builders. Other researchers have looked at the skill of the Nascan weavers, whose geometric patterns of birds and gods, warriors and animals survive. Weaving was clearly a well developed and highly regarded art. Any weaver understands the principle of designing a pattern small on a grid system and multiplying it up into a larger pattern. This skill could easily be transferred from the loom to the desert floor.

The work of other researchers has suggested that even this explanation is too complicated. Professor Anthony Aveni of Colgate University and his team of a dozen volunteers made a pretty passable small imitation Nasca trapezoid with attached spirals, simply designing by eye and using string and boxes to remove the stones, all in 90 minutes. Professor Aveni calculated that at this quite comfortable pace, a team of 100 Nascans could have cleared a typical trapezoid in two days.

But if careful archaeological detective work and imaginative attempts to recreate the Lines have demolished some of the mystery surrounding them, the biggest puzzle of all remains: why did the Nascans build them?

The alien space-craft theory may have been popular with the general public, but since the 1940s one theory has dominated among researchers: the Nasca Lines were a giant astronomical plan, pointing out constellations and enabling the Nascans to predict important dates in the annual calendar, such as the winter solstice.

This theory was made popular by a remarkable woman, Maria Reiche, who devoted her life to studying and then protecting the Lines. She came to live in Nasca in the 1940s and never left. By day she trekked across the pampa examining Lines, by night she lived in frugal circumstances. Locals idolised her for putting Nasca on the map and for her fierce energy when it came to protecting the monuments. She was convinced the meaning of the Lines was incredibly complicated – and built on an extraordinary knowledge of the stars and constellations that she believed the Nascans had.

But astronomer Jaroslav Kokocnik, from the Czech Academy of Sciences, puts his finger on the problem with this hypothesis. It is certain that some of the Lines appear to connect with the moon, the sun and other celestial bodies. Some Lines do point to sunrise and sunset at the summer and winter solstice. It is clear that these dates would have been important to an agricultural community, especially one so dependent on meagre supplies of water. 'But,' he says, 'there is a problem with the theory. There are many lines and many stars, and so matching them up becomes too complicated.' With a wry smile Kokocnik continues, 'And there's another problem which I will show you at sunset.'

Sure enough, as the sun sets the dryness of the atmosphere and the regular afternoon wind combine to blow up a light suspension of dust in the atmosphere. In the dim light and with the horizon obscured, it is more or less impossible to see where the Lines are pointing. And up above there are a million stars and hundreds of constellations, almost any one of which can be matched to one of the hundreds of shapes and lines and spirals on the pampa.

Aurelio thinks he may have the answer. He decided to take a look at the first written accounts of Peruvian coastal culture – by the Spanish chroniclers in the sixteenth century. These accounts were written nearly 1,000 years after the Nascans themselves vanished from the pampa, but Aurelio still found intriguing references to the Lines.

The chroniclers described three different kinds of activities associated with the Lines. The straight lines – many of which seem to lead to the tops of the mountains – were used for ritual processions. The trapezoids were used for ritual races. The third activity took place in that the big drawings of animals and birds were used for ritual dances. Aurelio believes that this is the true explanation of why the Nascans built the Lines.

There is indeed something extraordinary about the drawings. Take the huge spider monkey. The line of the drawing starts below its tail and then continues up into the spiral of the tail, along its arched back and round its head, down into the left arm and round each one of its five fingers, up and then down into its right hand, continuing on unbroken along the line of its belly and its back legs to terminate in a line running parallel to the beginning line. To walk, the monkey is 1.5 kilometres of sandy trail and never once does the walker cross his own path. The same is true of many of the other drawings. It is easy to see how the Nascans could have danced or processed along the figures in some ritual activity. And Reindel has found the sand inside these figures compacted exactly as it would be had they been frequently used for such an activity.

But given that the drawings were built at quite different times – and given that they were possibly used for quite different purposes many hundreds of years after they were built, the evidence of the sixteenth-century chroniclers does not guarantee much of an insight into the minds of the long-vanished Nascans.

Markus Reindel will not speculate. Of one thing, though, he is sure. If we are ever to understand the meaning of the Lines then it is crucial that we struggle to understand what made the Nascans tick – try to get inside their heads and so comprehend their world view.

The shocking evidence of the Cahuachi skulls helps in the journey towards that understanding. The Nascans were very different from us. They did not see the world the way we see it. They did not even see the landscape we see: a desert plain, cut by eroded river valleys and young spiky mountains raised high by tectonic activity, and as a result subject to regular earthquakes. To the Nascans, theirs was a sacred landscape, created by mythical creatures and conveying messages we can only guess at. Their movement around and across that landscape was a crucial part of their ritual life and their understanding of their place in the world. To get to grips with the Lines we must certainly try to comprehend this. They were surely built for a reason but we should not expect to be able to make their builders' logic fit ours. We may never be able to understand the Lines.

Reindel is certain of one thing: water played a crucial role in the survival of the Nascan civilisation. According to him, 'The constant factor – which is like a guideline in our investigation – is water. Water must have been the central point in the life of the people here, in this extreme ecology.'

How did they manage to live here? 1,500 to 2,000 years ago, when the Nascans lived here on the pampa, the climate and environment were every bit as harsh as they are today. How did they survive? For one thing, they built an amazing network of underground tunnels and aqueducts that brought water to the dry pampa. These water courses are still in use today.

Water is the key to understanding this culture.

And one researcher – not an archaeologist, not an astronomer, not even an anthropologist, but an inspired amateur – believes that it is water that provides the key to explaining the mystery of the Lines.

David Johnston is a retired school teacher from the United States who came to Nasca first as a tourist. The local priest, an American missionary, told him how severe the water shortage was in Nasca town and David, who had had some luck dowsing for water in the past, decided to give it a go in Nasca. He selected a place he thought would be good and when the locals dug, they hit fresh water. They called it 'the miracle well' and asked David to come back the following year.

It was the next year that, out dowsing again, he made the discovery that was to spark off a passion that has come to rule his life: 'As I came up over a hill, tracing a water source that I knew existed there and looking at a fault in front of me, here was this geoglyph system pointing the course of what I was following. And at that point you just hyperventilate. You sit down, you look around and you say, "My God! I think I've got something here." '

At that moment, sitting on the hill in the desert, David had made a connection: between water and the drawings in the sand. But it is not a simple connection or an obvious one.

For more than five years now he has been returning to Nasca, amassing the evidence to support his theory. It has become a passion. He has walked hundreds of kilometres, following the rivers right the way up to the base of the Andes and walking back west down as far as the Pacific coast. And all the time he is looking for the three things that together make up his theory: water sources, geological faults and those enigmatic marks on the ground.

On his own or with a guide from Nasca, Johnston has frequently found himself walking for two or three days through the harshest of lands. As he says, this is 'literally a sterile desert, and once you get out on that desert there is absolutely no vegetation, no living creatures, nothing … It's a very, very hazardous area. Mobile phones don't work here. There are no roads, no water supplies, no one to come and help. You're on your own.'

His interest is far from simply an academic urge to understand these Lines, these curiosities. For Johnston the Lines are a kind of message from the past, a clue that could help today's Nascans live a better life. As he trudges the desert in the dust and the glaring heat, following lines in the dirt, chasing faults, searching for evidence of hidden water, he will come across hamlets – a couple of houses here, there, a single family, camped out in a kind of tent attached to a single tree. Whenever he asks why these lonely communities are so small, the answer is always the same. There simply isn't enough water to survive. Yet time after time, just a short way from these lonely modern homesteads Johnston would find evidence of ancient Nascan settlements – the remains of substantial houses, farm buildings, graveyards – communities that had clearly supported dozens of people in these very same places at a time when the climate was just as dry. These long dead Nascans *must* have been able to get enough water to survive.

This has given Johnston a high respect for the long vanished Nascans. He believes the Lines are 'a water utilities map of the desert' which was used to enable the Nascans to live well here 2,000 years ago and which could be used to help their present day descendants live a better life. He says, 'We're using all sorts of modern scientific equipment – everything from satellites to remote sensing to geophysical and water analysis equipment – to understand what they knew, what they utilised within these valleys and marked with the lines in Nasca.'

As he gathered more and more examples that supported his hunch, David began to develop a more refined hypothesis. The trapezoids showed where concentrated flows of water existed below ground – they were a kind of permanent marker of where water could be found. Smaller triangles marked where water-bearing faults existed on valley sides. Spiral markings were for places without water.

Well-intentioned as his researchs were, the initial reaction of the local people to his theory was hostile. There's a bit of a tradition of people who go against the orthodoxy being run out of Nasca. Martha Reiche, it is rumoured, would arrange for researchers with opinions that ran counter to hers to be arrested! So Johnston decided to keep quiet.

But he did not give up. He simply reasoned that he needed academic support for his hunch before it could be used to help the local people. Being neither an archaeologist nor a hydrologist nor a geologist, he knew he risked being shot down in flames or simply ignored. So he worked away doggedly until he had acquired sufficient information for someone somewhere to take his theory seriously.

That person was Steve Mabee, a hydrologist from the University of Massachusetts, a specialist in how water works its way through different rocks. He recalls, 'After looking at the satellite image and seeing all of the structures and the features and the faults that are quite visible on a satellite image, I was hooked. Without question. And I said, "This is a worthwhile idea that should be tested." '

In November 2001 the pair were in Peru together, driving over the rough hot desert roads looking for more evidence.

For Steve, the bare rocky landscape where the Nascan civilisation flourished is a geologist's paradise: 'There are rocks and great exposures everywhere, and you have 100 per cent sunshine for 12 hours a day. No rain, no bugs, and a nice breeze comes up in the afternoon. What could be better?'

He and David Johnston tour the pampa in a four-wheel drive searching for the evidence necessary to test David's hunch in a way that satisfies Steve, a self-confessed sceptic. Working with geophysical methods and the time-honoured geologist's method of using your eyes, Steve is mapping the geology of the pampa – looking for faults and the sparkling evidence in the rock of minerals like quartz that show water once flowed there.

The Earth's crust is broken into many pieces, which geologists call plates. Peru is at the margin of two of them: the Nasca plate and the great South American plate. These two huge fragments of the Earth's crust are moving towards each other at the rate of eight millimetres a year. It doesn't sound like much but over a million years that works out at eight kilometres. The Nasca plate is made up of oceanic material and so, being denser and heavier, it is disappearing under its neighbour. But as it sinks under the South American plate, the Earth's surface, like a giant rug, is being creased and crumpled and forced up into ridges. Tremendous heat is generated by this movement and as a result there are volcanoes all down the western side of South America. The whole area is also subject to earthquake activity as the two plates rub against each other, stick and give way. Four-fifths of the small town of Nasca was levelled in 1996 when an earthquake struck. All this folding and seismic activity also means that this area is riddled with faults and fractures running through the rock.

And it is these, David Johnston believes, that hold the secret to how the Nascans were able to obtain sufficient water to develop agriculture and a flourishing civilisation in such a bare and dry landscape.

Though hardly any rain falls on the pampa at all, not far to the east – less than an hour's drive today – rise the Andes, 3,000 metres high. Snow-covered all the year round, these mountains are an area of high precipitation. Snow melt and rain run in rivers down to the coast during the winter months. But in the southern part of the Nascan area, the rivers dry up for most of the year so farmers cannot depend on them for irrigation.

But the water from the highlands can also reach Nasca by another route. Up in the mountains, it trickles down through the soil into the rock. When it hits a geological fault in the rock, it can run along that fault. And because the difference in height between the Andes and the sea is so great, over quite a short distance, gravity exerts a strong pull over the water and it runs freely down, trickling and jumping through a series of fractures in the rock, ever downhill, heading towards the Pacific ocean. Sometimes this water will emerge from the fault on the side of a valley as a spring.

Mabee has studied the chemical signature of the water in springs in the Nasca area and has been able to show where the water originally came from and which rocks it has travelled through on its journey. This spring water has come from the high Andes. Because these springs are fed from the mountains and run underground, they are protected from evaporation, and so, Mabee believes, they are a much more consistent and reliable water source than the rivers. He has also analysed the water quality and found that it is much sweeter and cleaner than river water and so would be a much better and safer source of drinking water.

To survive in the harsh Nascan desert ancient people simply needed a good way of identifying and remembering where these reliable underground water sources were. Steve Mabee has no trouble believing that the Nascans had this knowledge: 'Living close to the land they would have been at the pulse of the landscape, understanding its rhythms. If water was always available from these springs, of course they would have followed the vegetation and lived there.'

He also believes they would have spotted the faults: 'Anybody who works the land is in tune with their land and they have good observational skills. It's just a natural thing ... You get this beautiful colourful malachite and quartz and you can see them going across the landscape ... They're visually appealing and you can't miss them.'

Mabee is trying to draw up a comprehensive map of the geological faults and the water sources in the area, just as Reindel is trying to note all the geoglyphs. Johnston is trying to match his evidence of geoglyphs, water courses and ancient Nascan settlements with Mabee's water-bearing geological faults. And in more than half the cases there is a close match. But Mabee is still uncertain if Johnston has really cracked the mystery of the Lines: 'I really don't know ... I think it's a very complicated book that we're trying to decipher here and I don't know if there's just one straight answer or one theory that's going to explain it all. If I was dying in the desert, and there was a sign that said, "Town. 50 kilometres that way" and then there was a trapezoid pointing to a water source, which way would I go? I'd probably go to town. At this point.'

If the true intentions of the Line builders still evade our understanding, there is another mystery about the Nascans that recent science has at last resolved. They flourished in this forbidding land. The elaborate network of underground aqueducts that they built still exists today, and David Johnston has shown that they knew how to use the natural springs to live in places where there is no rain and few streams. We know they had long distance trading connections and lived a relatively comfortable life. But by the sixth century their civilisation had disappeared. How and why did this happen?

Markus Reindel has found evidence at his site, Los Molinos, of a natural catastrophe that devastated the community. Around the third century AD this driest of parched deserts was ravaged by tremendous floods. Mudslides must have come careering down the ravine and swept away whole houses. It was probably the result of a catastrophic El Niño event, bringing – once in thousands of years – rainfall to Nasca. It seems to have been around this time that Line building fizzled out.

But worse was to come.

Professor Mike Baillie is a dendrochronologist from Queen's University, Belfast. Dendrochronology – the science of dating by the study of tree rings – is a recent scientific discipline that is proving itself to be an amazing tool for understanding all kinds of historical puzzles. Each ring on a tree is like a year in the calendar. The weather in that year leaves a similar mark in all trees of the same species. So, by matching back from a living tree today through overlapping timbers to sub-fossilised trees of the past, it has been possible to establish a continuous record of tree rings for many parts of the world that stretches back thousands of years. In Ireland, for instance, the record stretches back 7,400 years. The pattern of rings is now computerised so that if any new piece of timber is analysed and its pattern of rings – its fingerprint – matched against the master list in the computer, its exact date will emerge. Unlike carbon dating, dendrochronology gives a precise year, not a range of years.

By dendrochronology it has been possible to date precisely the famous Viking long boat, the Oseberg ship, and to show that it was built of Irish oak in the Viking town of Dublin. Dendrochronology has been used to prove that a Stradivarius violin was in fact a fake, as the wood dated from too late in the century. It has even been used to work out the date of one of the biggest earthquakes in history, the great Cascadia earthquake that rocked the north-west coast of North

America long before literate settlers arrived, some time in the winter of 1700.

In some parts of the world thin rings and wide rings can be matched precisely to rainfall and sunshine, and so, as well as giving dates to wooden artefacts and buildings, dendrochronology can help climate historians establish what the weather was like in a given year.

But Mike Baillie's Irish bog oaks are not so easy to read. 'The trouble is with European oaks in a temperate region, you can't just say, "Wide ring, it was warm and wet." What we can do is ... look and see the relative condition of the tree growth. We can say, "The tree really didn't like this" as opposed to, "Oh! The tree thought this set of conditions were fine." So what I've been doing for some time now is looking at some of the worst growth conditions in this long record. What we find (is) there are some very interesting dates coming out. These are times when the trees really go, "Oh! We did not like that!" '

The first really big event that Mike Baillie came across was 540 and 541. All over Northern Ireland he found that the oaks had a scar of damage for those years. 'We're not just talking about trees not liking their growth conditions, we're talking about physical damage of some kind,' he says.

And the more he looked at this event, the stranger it became. For a similar pattern of damage showed up right around the planet – from Europe to South

America and from North America to Siberia. Whatever happened at that time – the time the Nascan civilisation vanished – was a global environmental catastrophe of extraordinary proportions.

Data from ice cores drilled in South America suggest there was an extreme drought at this time. However, ice cores drilled in Greenland provide contradictory evidence.

Mike Baillie believes this event could have been a super volcano that threw up enough ash and chemicals to alter the global climate on a drastic scale. But he thinks another explanation is even more likely. He believes it could well have been an impact from space, a meteorite or a comet that collided with earth: 'It's the only event in the last two millennia that stands out in all the records. And that makes it a very unique event. As you look back in time, it's the worst event you come to first. That's a strange way to put it, but you're looking back, and you go, "Pah! What on earth was that?" … in terms of tree rings, it's a big and extremely classy event.'

Whatever it was, coming on top of the damage caused by earthquakes and huge floods, the global disaster of the mid sixth century was too much for the Nascans. They had survived 1,000 years, using their skill, their technical know-how and their powers of observation to build a rich and complex society in one of the least hospitable places on earth, but they could not survive this. Their settlements were abandoned;

their culture disappeared. They vanished, leaving only their mysterious pictures in the desert to baffle and beguile the peoples who came after them.

recent years Big Foot – or Sasquatch as the elusive creature is known in Canada
as been sighted five times here at Wolf Lake, British Columbia. Jeff Meldrum,
ofessor of anatomy at Idaho State University (top left – with footprint cast) and
ul Freeman (top right – with handprint cast) are part of the army of American
g Foot investigators who collect evidence of the creature's existence.

When the tomb of the boy pharaoh Tutankhamun was found in 1922 it caused a sensation. Egyptologist Dr Salima Ikram (inset, left) is one of the many academic fascinated by the secrets his tomb revealed. Though images and statues of the king (above) had been identified by Egyptologists, there was little other evidenc to lead them to his treasure-crammed tomb and in the 1920s, newspapers

...aimed the mysterious tomb had been protected by a curse, like the one written ... hieroglyphics on a tomb at Saqqara (top). So fascinated have people become by ...e tomb and its treasures that the Tutankhamun Exhibition in Dorchester, England ...bove) includes a reproduction of what Howard Carter found. This picture was ...ken during filming for the itv 1 series of **Incredible Stories**.

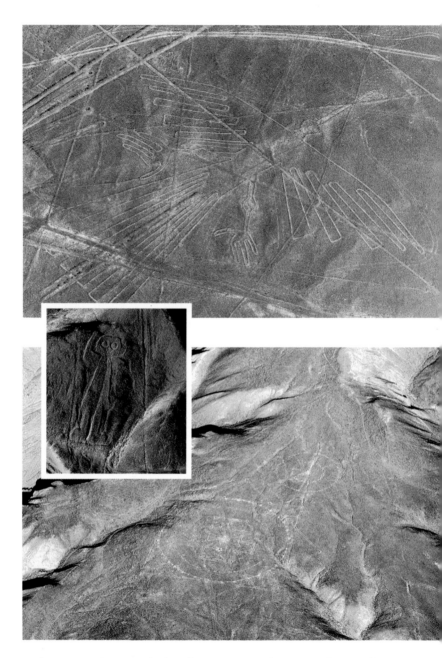

In the 1930s when people first flew across southern Peru they made an astonishing discovery. Written in the earth of this remote desert region were thousands of gigantic drawings: animals, insects, birds, long straight lines and odd geometric shapes. Some are large enough to be seen from space (top right)

...haeologists have established that they were made around 1,700 years ago by ...e Nasca culture. Argument still rages as to why the Nascans made these ...ricate and complicated pictures. The humanoid (inset left) has encouraged ...ne to think aliens were involved.

Peruvian archaeologist Aurelio Rodriguez has a theory that the patterns were use
for ritual dancing. Many of the drawings, including those of birds and animals (s
also page 4, top) are made of one continuous line that never crosses – permittin
processional dancing (top) as this speculative drawing by Rodriguez shows.

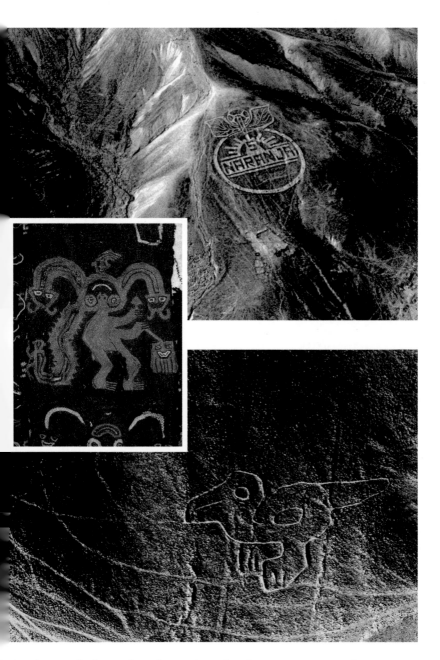

...king the geoglyphs is relatively simple and 20th century Peruvians have ...ised the advertising potential of the site (top right). The Nascans were skilled ...vers and potters and there is much similarity between the geoglyphs and the ...er images they made (inset).

The Peruvian pampa where the Nascan people lived until the 6th century AD is one of the driest places on earth. Scattered amongst the archaeological remains of their houses, temples and workshops are these tombs with dessicated bodies, many wrapped in beautiful woven fabrics, and some with extraordinary hair.

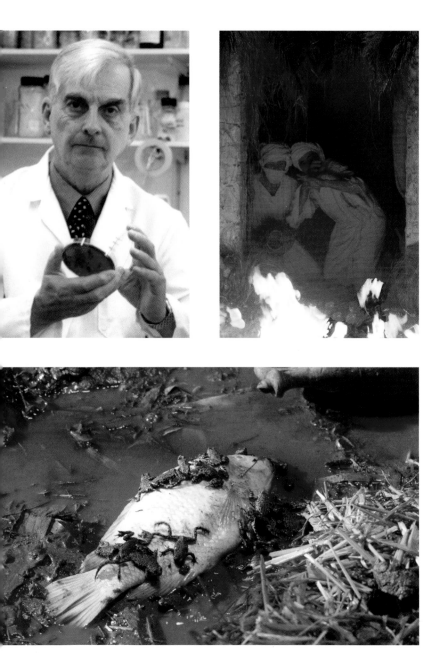

The Bible tells of ten amazing plagues that struck Egypt in the time of Moses. A blood red Nile and plagues of dead fish, frogs and mosquitoes were followed by devastating hail and locust swarms, and worse. Professor Hugh Pennington, a bacteriologist at Aberdeen University, (top left) can explain some of the plagues in terms of modern science. But for the itv 1 series, **Incredible Stories**, we had to recreate most of the plagues in the studio (above and top right.)

The legend of the lost city of Atlantis has haunted people for more than 2,500 years. As written by the ancient Greek philosopher Plato, it tells of an advanced civilisation that disappeared in a day and a night from some natural catastrophe. Now archaeology and volcanology have come together to suggest the origin of the legend. Knossos Palace (bottom left) was at the centre of the advanced Minoan

vilisation that flourished a thousand years before Plato. Minoans also controlled
the island of Santorini (bottom right) and recent excavations show earthquake
damage to the Minoan port of Akrotiri (top right). Volcanologist Dale Dominey
owes (inset) has investigated the huge eruption of 1628BC that enlarged the
olcano's caldera and changed the shape of Santorini island itself (top left).

Professor Alan Judd of Sunderland University (top right) has a theory that escapes of methane gas from the bottom of the sea may be responsible for the otherwise inexplicable loss of ships in places like the Bermuda Triangle. In December 2000 he led an expedition to an area of the North Sea known as the Witch Ground

ere there lies a fishing boat that might have been sunk by a gas escape.
ing him was Professor Robert Prescott of St Andrews University (bottom right,
eground). Their state-of-the-art survey ship was able to lower an ROV to the
bed (inset left) to examine the wreck up close.

Vampires are popularly associated with Transylvania (bottom left and right), a remote and rural part of Rumania. Folk stories about vampires from that region of Europe were incorporated by Irish author Bram Stoker into his novel **Dracula**. But American folklorist Michael Bell (top left) has discovered that the tracking down

...mpires was still a common folklore practise in North America in the 18th and ...th centuries. He has documented a large number of cases, including that of ...ercy Brown who was buried with her family in the churchyard at Essex, Rhode ...and (top right) in 1892.

The 'vampire' story of Mercy Brown and how she was dug up by her family and neighbours to stop her preying on her brother and father has been documented in detail by folklorist Michael Bell. Here members of a local theatre group on Rhode Island reconstruct the macabre events of that March afternoon for our cameras.

CHAPTER 4

The Ten Plagues of Egypt

O f all the episodes in the Bible, the story of the Ten Plagues of Egypt is among the most colourful – a series of flesh-creeping and disgusting plagues that descend, one after another, on the suffering people of Egypt.

The Nile turns to blood and then becomes clogged with dead and stinking fish; a plague of frogs followed quickly by plagues of lice and then flies. Revolting boils break out on man and beast, and hail and locusts together destroy the crops. Then, for three whole days and nights comes an eerie, total darkness – a darkness 'that can be felt'. And finally, the most horrifying curse of all, the universal death of the firstborn in every household, from that of the highest Pharaoh to that of his lowliest slave.

Highly dramatic, the story has all the makings of a spine-chilling horror movie. Yet scientific research now suggests that, far from being melo-dramatic, this is in fact a credible sequence of natural events that could well have happened, almost exactly as the Bible describes.

In the Bible, the horrifying series of Ten Plagues that afflicted Egypt is a crucial part of the story of how the Israelites were helped by God to escape from bondage in Egypt. Moses and Aaron, on God's instructions, repeatedly offer the Pharaoh a choice: let us go or suffer another plague. Nine times Pharaoh refuses to let the children of Israel go. Only after the tenth, and most horrific plague, does he finally agree to let Moses lead his people out of Egypt.

For many hundreds of years readers of the Bible neither questioned the story nor sought to understand it in more detail. But as biblical scholars began to look at how the Bible had been composed of various different documents, they came to the conclusion that the story of the Ten Plagues was the result of a number of different plague stories from different sources being combined. Scholars then suggested that *some* of the Plagues may have had some genuine basis in historical fact, but the collection of the ten together was to be understood more as an ancient saga – a story with some historical basis that had grown in the retelling. It was not really a journalistic account of what could actually have happened.

But since the 1950s more and more evidence has been accumulating, from microbiologists and hydrologists as well as from Egyptologists and biblical scholars, to suggest that the sequence of plagues as described in the Bible is in fact surprisingly realistic. Though to the modern reader the Plagues may appear to be unconnected, the sequence in fact follows a precise and very logical order. The order in which the Plagues come also, it turns out, makes sense in terms of the Egyptian seasons, starting in July-August and ending the following spring in late March or April – truly one ancient Egyptian *annus horribilis*.

The story of the Ten Plagues of Egypt begins in Exodus Chapter 7, when God commands Moses to tell Aaron to strike the River Nile with his stick, with horrifying consequences:

And Moses and Aaron did so as the Lord commanded; and he lifted up the rod and smote the waters that were in the river, in the sight of Pharaoh, and in the sight of his servants; and all the waters that were in the river were turned to blood.

And the fish that was in the river died; and the river stank, and the Egyptians could not drink of the water of the river; and there was blood throughout all the land of Egypt.

It has often been said that Egypt is 'the gift of the River Nile'. Without the river and its life-giving water, there would not be, and there would never have been, a prosperous country there. Even today, nine-tenths of the settlement of the country is in the Nile Valley, and in ancient times there were only scattered settlements out of the Valley, usually stone-quarrying communities. As Professor Kenneth Kitchen, Head of the Department of Egyptology at the University of Liverpool says, 'Where there's water, there's Egypt. There's life. There's vegetation. There's animals. There's mankind, humanity. If there's no water, there's nothing.'

The whole country's agriculture in former times was dependent on the water and the fertile silt the river brought. Before the building of the Aswan dam in the 1960s, this was delivered to Egyptian agriculture by the annual flooding of the River Nile. This flooding is the result of rainfall many hundreds of kilometres away in the highlands of Ethiopia and Uganda. The East African monsoon brings rain in the summer to this region. The amount of rain that falls is affected by among other things, the cyclical global weather event known as El Niño. Before the Aswan dam regulated the flow of water, the variation in rainfall also made for huge variation in the extent of this flooding. It ranged from 20 million cubic metres to 140 million cubic metres of water.

The ancient Egyptians knew how crucial the height of the Nile was to their prosperity. The extent of the country's agricultural land that could be cultivated in a given year depended on the flood height. In general, the higher the flood, the greater the potential harvest. The festival calendar was therefore linked to the height of the Nile, as was taxation. Egyptian officials devised a portable device to measure the flood height. Eventually they went on to build 'Nile-ometers' – towers with holes at different heights. As the Nile rose, it spilled through ever higher galleries of holes. They recorded the height on stone plaques, which were usually located in a central place, perhaps near a temple, so everyone could see what rate the taxes would be that year.

As a result of their obsession with tracking the behaviour of their river, as Professor Tony Brown from Exeter University explains, we have a detailed record of the behaviour of the Nile, stretching back thousands of years. He says: 'The Egyptians have recorded the height of the Nile, so we know a tremendous amount about its past levels, far more than we do for nearly any other river. They started recording around about 3000 BC, so from these recordings we've got some idea of the hydrology over the last 5,000 years. What they tell us is that we have had predominately dry conditions, but there have been periods when there have been large floods.'

A high Nile was good in many ways because more land could be cultivated, but extensive flooding could also be damaging. Houses, which were made of mud brick, were damaged by the water. Sediment would also come into homes and cause damage. The carcasses of dead animals and sewage would be washed into villages, homes and fields. If the water was unable to drain away, pools of standing water could develop, breeding grounds for mosquitoes and disease. A very high Nile was therefore a mixed blessing, but a low Nile spelled famine, and so disaster.

With the annual inundation being so crucial, its occurrence – or failure – took on enormous significance in political and religious, as well as economic, life. Egyptologist Aidan Dodson of Bristol University explains: 'The king was regarded as a god, was the god on earth. And part of his role was to ensure that the inundation happened when it did. Clearly if there was an unsuccessful inundation there would be (thought to be) ... some kind of problem with the king – whether because he was illegitimate, or insufficiently successful. So, clearly, if you do have a problem with the inundation – too much or too little – the first person who gets blamed is the king.'

The first plague, in which the Nile turns to blood, therefore struck at the heart of Egypt's life and livelihood. The colour of the cursed Nile is highly symbolic. Green – like their fertile river valley – was symbolic to the ancient Egyptians of life, wealth, prosperity. Red, on the other hand, was the colour of the desert. It stood for famine, danger and death.

Ken Kitchen expands on this idea: 'Red, of course, is a colour of ill omen in Egypt ... It's the colour of the god of tribulation and upset ... A red Nile, to start with, is a bad colour. It's a rogue Nile. Is this red Nile going to overcome us? Are we all going to be destroyed? Are we going to go hungry? Is it going to poison us? Or is it something that's come and it will go? ... If it doesn't, then the red Nile is fatal.'

It's plausible then that plague number one is a

symbolic disaster. However, there is another explanation for why there might have been a red Nile. As the ancient record indicates, the norm in ancient Egypt was fairly dry conditions. But when rainfall in the highlands of Ethiopia is exceptionally high, large amounts of red earth are scoured from the hillsides there. This sediment is carried all the way downstream to Egypt, making the high flooding Nile a red colour. This red inundation takes place in July or August. Professor Brown thinks this could be one explanation of the 'bloody Nile': 'One interpretation of that certainly is that it's a flood where suspended sediment was particularly red and that suspended sediment gets plastered all over the valley. It enters houses and it's extremely difficult to remove; it causes staining. It's a problem.'

There is, though, another explanation for the nightmare the Bible describes. And what makes this explanation the most likely is that it would, quite naturally, set in train a sequence of events that would lead to the other plagues.

The Nile, like many other water courses, sometimes suffers from highly toxic explosions of tiny plants known as algal blooms. These are made up of single-celled plants called flagellates, which are so small in themselves they are invisible to the naked eye. If the right combination of nutrients, light and temperature comes together, then the flagellates can multiply very rapidly. And if there are enough in a stretch of water, then it will turn a deep blood red. A very high Nile contaminated with large quantities of flagellates could have spread as a blood red flood across the inhabited part of Egypt.

While the flagellates keep growing, the Nile becomes ever redder. But eventually the environmental conditions start to change. Then the flagellates start to die in large numbers. Bacteria attack the dead vegetation, releasing chemicals that contaminate the water. It becomes scummy and foul, smelling bad and tasting unpleasant. No wonder, as the Bible says, the Egyptians 'could not drink of the water'. No wonder they desperately dug in the ground to find water fresh enough to drink.

But when an algal bloom contaminates a river, the turbid, smelly water is only the beginning. The breakdown of the algae by the bacteria may produce toxins that kill the fish and then a vicious cycle begins. Bacteria begin to feed on the dead fish. This lowers the oxygen level in the water, which makes conditions even more difficult for the surviving fish so that more of them die. Soon the whole ecosystem of the river gets out of balance. Fish are not the only species affected. Frogs quickly leave the contaminated river searching for fresh water, new supplies of food and cool, damp places where they can survive.

Evidence exists that a high, red Nile was not unknown to the ancient Egyptians. It is in a papyrus document known as the lamentations of Ipoweyo. No one knows if it is history or fiction, but the papyrus gives a vivid account of life in Egypt when it is in the grip of some kind of disaster. When the river is blood, the people of Upper Egypt are driven to despair. The land becomes a wasteland. Towns are ravaged. People flap about like fish and, at the end of their tether, simply let themselves be eaten by the crocodiles, rather than struggle on.

The most obvious and immediate result of the blood Nile, though, would have been frogs everywhere, and this is indeed, in the biblical account the plague that comes next:

And Aaron stretched out his hand over the waters of Egypt; and the frogs came up, and covered the land of Egypt. Exodus Chapter 8

It is part of the reproductive cycle of some species of Egyptian frog that they leave the Nile and come up onto land in large numbers. But this was something different. With the Nile contaminated, every surviving frog would have left the river. They came to infest the countryside in huge numbers. Like the rats in the story of the Pied Piper of Hamelin, they hopped about in the fields and came into the villages. They even infested houses and storerooms. When they died, the people were able to gather them into great piles where, the Bible says, they stank.

And now came the Third Plague. According to the

King James version of the Bible, this was a plague of lice that Aaron produced from the dust. Humans and animals were bothered by these lice. However, more recent translations of the Bible suggest that 'mosquitoes' would be a better translation. Scholars in the time of King James would not have been familiar with the fauna of Egypt and so would simply have picked a small insect with which they were familiar. Mosquitoes are a common problem in Egypt but with the Nile having flooded so widely, there would have been more water than usual in the valley. Once the monsoon finished in Africa, the river would have begun to retreat back to within its banks, leaving pools of standing water everywhere. Such pools of standing water are ideal breeding grounds for mosquitoes. Soon swarms of the irritating and deadly insects would have been coming into people's homes, whining and biting. Compared to a normal year, this would have been an epidemic.

The first three plagues, therefore, are all the natural consequence of an extremely high inundation of the Nile. In the cosmology of the time, troubles were expected to come in threes. So it is no surprise that the three 'water' plagues are followed by three on land.

The Bible says that the Children of Israel were at this time slaves in Egypt, working on big building projects for the Pharaoh. He is never named. It is difficult to know just when the Israelites were living in Egypt and what conditions were like for them.

However, little pieces of the jigsaw are gradually falling into place. Professor Kitchen likens the task before the historians who are trying to assemble this jigsaw to trying to tell the story of Britain today solely from what is written on stone inscriptions. He does believe, however, that the story of Exodus can be dated to the thirteenth century BC.

For the past 20 years Dr Edgar Pusch of Hildesheim Museum in Germany has been excavating the remains of an enormous town in the Egyptian delta that was the second capital of Ramesses II, the Pharaoh who dominated the thirteenth century. Ken Kitchen describes him as the Queen Victoria of ancient Egypt, who reigned for a long time and covered his country with major building works and monuments: 'A big fellow in every sense, he reigned for 66 years. He had eight principal queens. He had over 100 known children. He covered Egypt with monuments … He was spectacular in every way – a very theatrical Pharaoh. He was determined to make his mark, to please the gods and be glorious in Egypt as no other king had ever done. He was going to surpass everybody.'

Kitchen believes that it was this impressive new city that the Israelites were engaged in building at the time of Exodus. Covering around 40 square kilometres of land, it was at its apogee perhaps the largest city of the ancient world. It was a city with the hovels of the poor and the palaces of the rich. Dr Pusch has excavated administrative buildings, quays for boats to tie up, stables and temples, a goldsmiths' workshop. Then, in around 1130, the Nile changed its course and the city was abandoned. The stone buildings were used as quarries for stone while the mud buildings simply melted back into the mud of the Delta. It was not found again by archaeologists until the twentieth century.

Dr Pusch is constantly struck by what a colourful place it must have been at its height: 'We keep finding key stones which have the brightest colours you could imagine. It's not only the white of the limestone and the red of the granite. You have the blue and you have the green. You have the gold plated things, and (they were) trying to imitate gold and silver also by painting the door posts … So it must have been a very, very colourful picture in front of a green background, because the Delta is green just jumping to your eyes.'

It seems from the record that the Egyptians were content, even proud, to have to use foreign forced labour to complete their grand building projects. Egyptologists can also establish what it would have been like to work as a building labourer on cities such as this, as the Bible says the Israelites were. There are lots of colourful details from ancient Egypt of working conditions. Overseers had a quota to reach, and they would have used whipping to fulfil that quota. Writer Christine El Mahdy describes the conditions: 'In the summer in Egypt you're talking (temperatures in) the 50s°C. You're going down to the Nile to collect the mud. It's got to be carried up to the site. You've got the straw to go and collect from the fields. It's back-breaking work. It's the most awful pain, the most awful heat. We don't know very much about the limitations of work times. I mean you think about a nine-to-five working day – there's no doubt that didn't really apply in ancient Egypt.'

From the evidence of skeletons that have been examined by forensic archaeologists it seems clear that workmen had a very hard life. They had wear in their joints, bad backs and arthritis. They had parasitic infections and eye problems. They had amputations, the result perhaps of accidents. They had almost completely worn down teeth, for the sand in the bread rubbed their teeth like sandpaper. The additional problem for the Israelites, in Christine El Mahdy's opinion, was that they were naturally herdsmen who found themselves forced to work in the building trade. It was not really their metier.

No wonder, as the story of Exodus goes, it felt like slavery to them. No wonder they were desperate to escape.

Following the three water plagues, God helps Moses and Aaron bring three land plagues. The first of these was one of flies. As it says in Exodus Chapter 8:

There came a grievous swarm of flies into the house of the Pharaoh, and into his servants' houses and into all the land of Egypt: the land was corrupted by reason of the swarm of flies.

Professor Thomas Pennington is a microbiologist at Aberdeen University. He is intrigued by the Plague of flies. Just as the blood-red Nile can be shown to cause the next two plagues, Pennington believes this fourth plague can be shown to have a similar causal link with plagues five and six.

Moses is told to tell the Pharaoh:

> Behold the hand of the Lord is on thy cattle which is in the field, upon the horses, upon the asses, upon the camels, upon the oxen, upon the sheep: there shall be a grievous murrain.

And after the animals have been attacked by this disease ('murrain' is a general word for a pestilence or disease), the sixth plague visits skin boils on the unfortunate people of Egypt.

As Professor Pennington points out, Egypt has always suffered from plagues of flies. On occasions people have even been suffocated by enormous numbers of flies, and the dust from dead flies causes high rates of asthma there. But he does not think this biblical plague was of any ordinary fly. The key to understanding is in what comes next, for the swarms of flies can be directly connected with the murrain in cattle and the boils in people. There *is* a disease that can be spread by flies and that affects both animals and humans: it's called anthrax.

Anthrax has a fearsome reputation, all the more so

following the terrorist attacks of September 11th, when it was used to spread panic across America. It is used as a weapon of biological warfare because it is an extraordinarily persistent organism that can survive in the right environment – which is heat and moisture – for hundreds of years. Compared to other bacteria it is almost impossible to destroy. In Britain it used to be known as 'the woolsorters' disease', for people would catch it from imported wool. If anthrax spores are inhaled, they can get into the heart and lungs, and frequently the person dies.

However, skin anthrax is less deadly. It is generally spread by the spores getting into the bloodstream through a small cut or an insect bite. The word 'anthrax' comes from the Greek for coal, because the most dramatic part of skin anthrax is an intense coal-black hole surrounded by blisters and swelling. Because anthrax spores can survive so long, the organism is not evolving at a fast rate. Indeed, people or animals becoming infected with anthrax today may be being infected by spores that are as much as 200 years old. For this reason, anthrax today is indistinguishable from anthrax in medieval descriptions of the disease, so we can be pretty confident of what these ancient Egyptian boils would have looked like – in Professor Pennington's words, 'very, very dramatic. It's the sort of thing that would make a very big impact. Particularly if large numbers of people were getting this kind of boil.'

Nor is he surprised by the Bible's description of some people suffering from this plague and others not: 'It's very, very easy to come up with a scenario where one part of a country – for example the part of the country inhabited by the Israelites – has got a lower anthrax problem than the part inhabited by the Egyptians.'

Anthrax can be transmitted from one animal to another, or from animals to humans by contact, and also by flies. In Egypt there are some insects that specialise in biting the legs of animals and that transmit anthrax this way. This biting fly breeds in marshy ground. It would therefore have been much commoner by the Nile than in drier parts of the country. So the risk of contracting anthrax would have been different depending on which part of Egypt people lived in. It is also a fly that flourishes when there is a large amount of decaying matter around, as there is when the flooding Nile retreats inside its banks in the autumn.

The next three plagues are a trio of 'sky' plagues – all natural events which do happen in Egypt. What was special about them and what turned them from a problem into a disaster was how extreme they were and how each followed swiftly on the heels of the other. The first was hail:

And the Lord rained hail upon the land of Egypt. So there was hail and fire mingled with the hail, very grievous, such as there was none like it in all the land of Egypt since it became a nation. And the hail smote throughout all the land of Egypt all that was in the field, both man and beast; and the hail smote every herb of the field and brake every tree of the field.'

Hailstones grow inside the great anvil-headed clouds called cumulonimbus. Tremendous thunderstorms involve great disturbance in the atmosphere. Within thunderclouds, there are powerful updrafts and downdrafts. Water droplets are hurled upwards until they freeze. As they descend again, the outside of the droplets starts to melt. Then, hitting another updraft, the pieces of ice refreeze, growing bigger. Each droplet can be tossed up and down numerous times, each time growing a new layer of ice until, if you cut a hailstone open, it looks like an onion. The faster the winds within the clouds, the larger hailstones can grow. When these updrafts reach a speed of 100 mph, hailstones as big as 7½cm across can be formed.

As the residents of Sydney, Australia, discovered in early 1999, when a freak hailstorm smashed roofs and windows, pummelled cars and proved to be Australia's costliest natural disaster, such hail is not a minor event. People have even been killed by hail, and farmers in many parts of the world – including the dessert grape-growing areas of South Africa – take out special hail insurance because of the way hail can, in a matter of moments, destroy an entire crop. In the

United States, in the states of North and South Dakota, which lie in an area known as 'hail alley', the power of hailstorms to damage crops is so great that farmers club together to pay for 'hail-busting' planes. These fly high into the atmosphere when thunder storms threaten and 'seed' the clouds with silver nitrate. This can sometimes head off the development of a hail-producing storm, making it rain instead. Though such devastating hailstorms are not common in Upper Egypt, they do happen.

This one, which destroyed the flax and barley crops, was swiftly followed by even worse – plague number eight, a plague of locusts.

Swarms of locusts tend to arrive in Egypt in February or March. Writer Christine El Mahdy recalls quite how horrifying the arrival of a plague of these insects can be: 'When a swarm of locusts appeared over the horizon it would almost appear like a black cloud, rather like a thunder cloud ... a wall that was simply coming towards you. When the locusts arrived, they were so thick you could barely breathe for the locusts around you. As they pass through, they literally devour everything. They leave nothing but stalks in their wake. It's really quite appalling.'

The Bible describes the plague of locusts:

For they covered the face of the whole earth so that the land was darkened; and they did eat every herb of the land, and all the fruit of the trees which the hail had left; and there remained not any green thing in the trees or in the herbs of the field through all the land of Egypt.

The crops of the Egyptian farmers had been devastated by hail and then stripped to the bare twigs and stalks by the huge swarms of locusts. Now came the third sky plague:

And the Lord said to Moses, Stretch out thine hand toward heaven that there may be darkness over the lands of Egypt, even darkness which may be felt.

And Moses stretched forth his hand toward heaven; and there was a thick darkness in all the land of Egypt three days.

They saw not one another, neither rose any from his place for three days ...

This overpowering darkness might have been an eclipse of the sun, or even a vast cloud of ash thrown up by a volcano. But the only active volcano close enough to have made it dark in the middle of the day is Santorini. Its big eruption – which would have been seen from Egypt – has now been dated to 1628 BC (see Chapter 5), too early for the accepted twelfth century BC date of Exodus.

However, Professor Brown thinks the most likely explanation for this plague is a sandstorm. In Egypt, these intense storms blow enormous quantities of dust and sand up into the atmosphere and make it extremely difficult to move around or even see. They are indeed a darkness that can be felt and are memorably unpleasant to live through. Sandstorms damage the crops, but they also become more common after there has been crop failure. Professor Brown says: 'For example, if we have a period of drought, so that the crops die, then the strength of the soil is decreased because the roots of the crops are dead and so the result of that is that soil can be blown much more easily.'

The third sky plague, therefore, came as a consequence of the first two. But the really interesting point about these three plagues is the evidence they provide of when they happened. The story goes that the flax was still in the fields but the wheat was not high enough to be damaged. This locates the devastating hailstorm in early February. It was followed swiftly by the swarms of locusts. Late February to early March is the worst time in Egypt for locusts. Sandstorms come in March or April with the Khamsin wind. The worst sandstorm of the year – in a year when drought, or in this case hail and locusts, mean the soil is loose and ready to be blown about – is usually the first one, so it is likely that this plague struck in March.

Far from being random, therefore, these three plagues follow a natural seasonal sequence. So is that true of the earlier six plagues, too?

Professor Ken Kitchen is certainly convinced. In his

view, the plagues, starting with the first and ending with the tenth, took place over one catastrophic year. The first plague – the blood-red Nile, undrinkable, smelly and full of dead fish – took place with the flooding in July or August. 'Then,' says Kitchen, 'the consequences all follow' – the plagues of frogs and the plagues of mosquitoes. According to Kitchen, 'That takes us through the autumn into the winter.' When the fifth plague came and attacked the cattle, the story states that some were still in the byres while others were out in the fields. According to contemporary agricultural practice in Egypt, cattle were kept indoors from May to December. In January they began to be taken out into the fields. So the fifth plague must have fallen on the Egyptians in January. Kitchen says, 'With the hail, and the flax and barley coming up, we're definitely into February … and the hail crashing down is the beginning of the end.'

The eighth plague – the locusts – came in February-March, and the ninth, the sandstorm, hit in the same month.

What Aidan Dodson finds interesting about the story of the plagues, is the way each one is so closely connected with agriculture, the lifeblood of the Egyptian state: 'The plagues are very interesting because they are clearly related to the major problems that the civilisation faced. They're focused at its economic base, at agriculture.'

Professor Tony Brown points to another aspect of how

the story of the plagues is told – over the five chapters of Exodus – that suggests it is based on things that really happened: 'There are small aspects of the narratives which also indicate that it's based on observations. For example, the fact that some of the events were dismissed because the Pharaoh said that his magicians could do it, and others weren't. The fact that the magicians said, Well, they could do it – we can also read that as saying, Well, they'd occurred before, so them being created by Moses means nothing because they'd been observed before. So there are small clues within Exodus itself that suggest that these are actually based on observations of real events for the most part.'

But that leaves the final plague – the most horrifying and deadly, and the hardest to explain scientifically. The story is told in Exodus Chapter 12:

And it came to pass that at midnight the Lord smote all the firstborn in Egypt, from the firstborn of the Pharaoh that sat on his throne unto the firstborn of the captive that was in the dungeon; and the firstborn of the cattle ... and there was a great cry in Egypt; for there was not a house where there was not one dead.'

The Israelites, according to the Bible, had previously been warned by God to paint their doors with blood. In this way God knew which homes to spare from this terrible curse on the firstborn.

From the first plague onwards, Moses and Aaron were trying to persuade the Pharaoh to let the people of Israel leave Egypt. The plagues were a way of twisting his arm. But, the story goes, it was only after this tenth plague that Pharaoh finally decided to let the Israelites go. Is there any possible scientific explanation for such an event – the death of the firstborn child in every household?

Greta Horst, the scholar whose seminal article in the 1950s started people thinking that the Ten Plagues might actually have been based on fact, suggested that the word had been mis-translated. The death of the firstborn, she wrote, was in fact the loss of the first fruits – the wheat harvest. But would this have been bad enough to change the Pharaoh's mind and persuade him to let the Israelites leave Egypt? After the other crops had been so effectively destroyed by the locusts and the sandstorm, perhaps the loss of the wheat harvest too was the straw that finally broke the Pharaoh's resolution. But it does seem surprising that it should have had this dramatic effect on the Pharaoh.

Recently an American microbiologist claimed that, given the shortage of food after the previous plagues, the eldest son in each household might have been given additional rations compared to the rest of the family. If there were any contamination of the food, therefore, eldest children would have been disproportionately affected. However, Egyptologists tend to dismiss this argument as unlikely.

Christine El Mahdy searches for a slightly different explanation. She sees the tenth plague not as something to be taken literally but as symbolic of some kind of violent battle that happened at the time the Israelites left Egypt and that resulted in a lot of bloodshed. This leads her to place the Exodus story shortly after the time of Tutankhamun, when his successor Horemheb was Pharaoh. She believes his campaign to eliminate references to Tutankhamun from historical monuments did not stop at chiselling away the boy Pharaoh's name cartouches. She believes there was violence and ethnic cleansing on a large scale and it is this that is recorded in the horrors of the tenth plague.

However, most scholars place Exodus at the time of Ramesses II. If there had been some cataclysmic violent conflict at that time, why does it not appear in the historical record?

Despite the many fascinating details that we do know about life in ancient Egypt, the fact is our knowledge is based on scant evidence, and it is coloured by what the Egyptians chose to record. It is very hard to know about the bad things that happened in ancient Egyptian times. Unlike the Chinese, who from the earliest time made detailed accounts of earthquakes, floods, solar eclipses and other natural disasters that affected their country, the Egyptians took care to avoid mentioning such things. They believed that if you wrote something down it might magically come to pass. They even went so far as to alter certain hieroglyphs in tombs where the hieroglyph was of a creature like a snake or a bee, lest it come to life and harm the mummy in the tomb. Pharaohs were very interested in making monuments that recorded their triumphs; about their defeats they kept silent.

'A pharaoh will only celebrate victories. The pharaoh wins – up it goes,' comments Ken Kitchen. People who wage wars never lose, they always win victories. No Pharaoh would ever have reliefs on temple walls saying, "Here are my chariots being drowned in the water. Here's the foreign people getting away. I have been defeated." That is not acceptable to the gods of Egypt. If you have a defeat you shut up.'

Aidan Dodson thinks the Exodus story is a reworking of a historical event known as the expulsion of the Hiksos. If the Israelites and the Hiksos are one in the same people, then the historical record and the Bible differ on how the Israelites came to leave Egypt. In the Bible, the horror of the tenth plague eventually convinces Pharaoh that he will have no prosperity unless he releases the Israelites from bondage in Egypt. The Egyptian records tell a rather different story. They describe the Hiksos as a powerful people from Palestine who were not in bondage in Egypt but in control. Eventually the Egyptians managed to expel the Hiksos.

Aidan Dodson thinks this contradiction is easy to understand: 'One really only has to look at it almost as modern propagandistic retelling of wars by the losers.

You can imagine that this event of the Israelites and other related peoples, leaving Egypt in one large group, is going to be a major part of their folklore. It was an event which clearly happened. But round the campfire, when you're talking to the children, you don't tell them that you lived in Egypt for a hundred years ... and then finally the Egyptians got so fed up they threw us out. Of course, it turns round – perhaps gradually – to being: we were the oppressed in Egypt. Then we escaped ... So my view of this is probably the most credible explanation for the Exodus legend.'

However, Ken Kitchen considers there is enough archaeological evidence to connect the story of Exodus, the Israelites and the forced labourers who built Ramesses II's delta city. Their name appears on a monument from the twelfth century. It was put up by Ramesses II's son and announces a victory against a tribal group living in Palestine. Archaeologists are also finding evidence of new settlements, of a group of arrivals springing up in the same area of Palestine around this time.

Whatever the history and the explanation of the enigmatic tenth plague, the fascinating fact remains that hundreds of years later, when the story of the plagues came to be written down, it was written in a particular sequence. Thousands of years later, scientific information from a range of disciplines, some of which people at the time of the Plagues simply could not have known, can make perfect sense of that sequence.

To Professor Ken Kitchen, the conclusion is obvious: The Ten Plagues are 'a complete cycle – almost through the whole year – in the valley of the Nile, not out of the imagination'.

CHAPTER 5

The Lost City of Atlantis

For thousands of years a mysterious legend has gripped people's imagination.

It's the tale of a great civilisation – more ancient than Ancient Greece and far more advanced – a fabulous city surrounded by a rich and fertile land known as Atlantis.

Legend says that the city of Atlantis disappeared suddenly beneath the ocean waves in a single day and night, never to be seen again.

For more than 2,000 years enthusiasts have believed that the legend of Atlantis must have been based on a real civilisation and have wondered where Atlantis could have been sited. Explorers and adventurers have searched for the lost island and found nothing.

But now – at last – new research from the earth sciences can be brought together with marvellous archaeological discoveries to show that 'Atlantis' did indeed exist, that the fertile and wealthy island did indeed vanish in a matter of hours and that the remnant is still there to be seen today.

Enter the word 'Atlantis' into an Internet search engine and the chances are it will come up with nearly half a million hits. Many will be for management consultants, holiday resorts, designer bed linen, all trading on the powerful appeal of the name. But most will be directly connected with the ancient Greek legend of a vanished civilisation. More than 2,000 books have been written about Atlantis. Almost every year, it seems, some new expedition of Atlantis-hunters sets forth in the hope of finding the lost city; or a new theory, based on underwater exploration or satellite photography or the analysis of ancient languages, is brought out that points to yet another plausible location for the lost land.

There's a Russian who thinks it will be found by diving off the south-western coasts of the British Isles, for he is convinced that Atlantis was located on the continental shelf that surrounds Britain and Ireland. This is not as crazy as it sounds: this vast area of land would have been dry and doubtless inhabited in the Ice Age when so much of today's sea water was locked up in ice.

There's a Scotsman who believes Atlantis is the entire South American continent and the capital city was high on the Bolivian altiplano.

And he's in good company: as long ago as the seventeenth century, the writer Francis Bacon was also arguing that South America was 'Atlantis', while Queen Elizabeth's own astrologer, John Dee, named North America 'Atlantis' on his maps.

In the 1920s enigmatic British adventurer and explorer Colonel P Fawcett disappeared in the forests of the Amazon hunting for Atlantis. No one knows if he found any evidence of the place before he died.

Every Atlantis-hunter picks certain aspects of the legend to help anchor his quest. Many have homed in on the fact that Atlantis was supposed to be an island – and a large island at that – with one researcher suggesting it is to be found in Greenland, another in Sri Lanka and yet another in Spitzbergen.

Two American writers have argued in a recent book that Atlantis is waiting to be found under the ice of Antarctica, and there's a group of Londoners who believe it is not even necessary to search: the Lords of Atlantis come to them in spirit and they are able to channel their wisdom and advice to humans. They are not the only ones who believe Atlantis is not so much a lost archaeological city or an archaeological curiosity as an ancient civilisation that still has much to teach us.

There's a school of thought – started in the nineteenth century by an enterprising, scholarly and imaginative American Congressman called Ignatius Donnelly – that Atlantis was the first world civilisation, now sunk somewhere in the mid-Atlantic. This theory holds that the similarity between the cultures and architecture of ancient peoples revealed in the archaeological remains of places as far apart as Cambodia, Egypt, Mexico and Peru can be accounted for by the fact that all these cultures share a common ancestor: Atlantis. In the twentieth century enthusiasts took the idea further, suggesting that the source of the advanced culture found at Atlantis was extraterrestrial.

But where did the legend first come from? And why does it spawn such varied geographical locations among those who are eager to rediscover it?

The whole legend has grown from a story written down by the Ancient Greek philosopher, Plato. Two and a half thousand years ago he wrote two Dialogues, called Critias and Timaeus. In the Dialogues – which take place between Socrates and a group of his acolytes and are discussions about politics and social organisation – it is the young man named Critias who tells the story of Atlantis. The Critias dialogue was never finished, but in both the piece that bears his name and Timaeus the young man is at pains to tell Socrates and his friends that this is a true, not a tall, story. He heard it from a relative, who heard it from another relative, who heard it from a friend, who had been told the story by a priest in Egypt around 590 BC.

Atlantis, Critias carefully explains, was a large island, ruled by a family descended from the sea god Poseidon and his human wife. This state flourished 9,000 years before the time when he was relating the tale to his friends in Athens. It been handed down by word of mouth through the generations in Egypt and then written down by his relative and kept in their family. Critias explains how he had heard the story often as a child and that – between the two Dialogues – he had re-read it to remind himself of the details.

In the story, 'the great and wonderful empire' of Atlantis was engaged in a military campaign to conquer all the countries around the Mediterranean, including Egypt and those on the Greek peninsula. In Critias' tale, the Atlanteans are clearly imperialist bullies. The heroes in the story are the Athenians, who lead a confederation of allies against Atlantis and eventually find themselves fighting alone against the evil empire. While the war is still raging, the Atlanteans and their island home come to a very bad end. In a cataclysmic combination of earthquake and flood that lasts a single day and night, the entire civilisation of Atlantis vanishes into the depths of the sea, leaving only an impassable barrier of mud to mark where it had once been. This disaster was the work of the gods, angry that the Atlanteans had 'lost all virtue'.

So far, so urban myth. As in most urban myths, the story comes from 'a friend of a friend' – or in this case a friend of a relative of a relative. (This kind of story even fits into a category recognised by paranormal investigators: a FOAF case.) The supposed date of the Atlantis culture – nearly 10,000 BC – increases scepticism, too. There is no known archaeological evidence for an advanced civilisation existing anywhere on Earth 10,000 years ago. There was certainly no Athens then,

and not even many people living on the Greek peninsula.

The complete disappearance of an entire large island
in a single cataclysmic natural disaster, stretches credibility further.

However, archaeologist Colin MacDonald of the
British School at Athens, pinpoints one reason why the
Atlantis story has for so many centuries captured so
many people's imagination and convinced them that
Plato was not making the story up: 'Suddenly in the
middle of (the Dialogues), crops up this story of
Atlantis in some detail. This stands out as being quite
different from the general, the normal topics that
(Plato) would discuss, and it is related in great detail,
as though he had a precise source for this information.
Perhaps we should take more notice of this story
because it is so out of character and out of keeping with
the normal dialogues he was writing.'

For Plato – out of the mouth of Critias – gives
numerous details about the glory that was Atlantis,
details that are quite incidental to the point of the
wider story he is telling. Quite irrelevant – unless he
repeats them, because they simply happen to be true.

Atlantis was a huge island, 'greater in extent than
Libya and Asia', situated somewhere beyond Gibraltar,
in the Atlantic Ocean. The Atlanteans, Plato said, held
sway over countries within the Mediterranean,
including North Africa as far as Egypt. According to
him, 'They had such an amount of wealth as was never

possessed before by kings and potentates and is not likely ever to be again,' and a combination of the natural fertility of their island and foreign trade meant that they had everything they wanted.

The central part of the island was a flat plain measuring around 300 by 200 kilometres, sheltered on its northern side by mountains bigger and more beautiful, Critias claims, than any that existed in his time. This plain was criss-crossed by man-made irrigation canals that enabled two crops a year to be grown.

On the island there were precious metals to be excavated. Among the abundant wild life there were even elephants. Pulses, herbs, chestnuts, 'fragrant things … essences which distil from fruits and flower' all flourished in the fertile soil. They also had an exotic fruit that was obviously unfamiliar to Critias and that he was at pains to describe – 'the fruit having a hard rind, affording drink, meat and ointment'.

The island was not just unusual because of its size and wealth. Having been partly fashioned by a God (Poseidon himself, after he had fallen in love with the woman who would bear his sons), it had a curious geography. It was, in fact, not one island, but three round islands, one inside each other, divided by two circles of water and then surrounded by the Atlantic Ocean. A combination of the country's extraordinary wealth and the inconvenience of this watery geography meant that it had an impressive number of docks, harbours, canals, walls and bridges, as well as temples and palaces.

It is at this point, as Critias describes a geography that sounds in some ways quite fanciful, that he makes Atlantis more believable by going into quite extraordinary detail about these canals, giving depth and width, and length to the nearest Greek stade, or 182 metres. He even says how long the bridges over the canals were (one-sixth of a *stade*).

After going into chapter and verse about the canals and defensive walls, Critias goes on to describe the main city. He tells of how the buildings were made of red, white and black rock; and the great city walls were covered in precious metals, including tin and brass. The royal palaces were constantly improved and from generation to generation became more impressive and beautiful. He tells of horse racing, of numerous enormous statues of gods made of gold, and statues of gods riding on dolphins. In the city there were fountains of cold and of hot water and 'They made cisterns, some open to the heavens, others roofed over, to be used in winter as warm baths.' Bulls were an important part of the city's religious life, and they were ritually slaughtered by Atlantis' leaders. At the heart of the citadel was a holy temple dedicated to the gods, out of bounds to the ordinary people and surrounded by an enclosure of gold.

Packed within the city walls were the dense settlements of the ordinary citizens of Atlantis, and all along the canals and in the harbours were numerous boats and 'merchants coming from all parts ... (who) kept up a multitudinous sound of human voices, and din and clatter of all sorts, night and day'.

The whole state was justly governed by the descendants of Poseidon and his lady. It is clear from Plato's tale that the Atlanteans were literate. In the early days, according to Critias, 'They possessed true and in every way great spirits, uniting gentleness with wisdom in the various chances of life ... They despised everything but virtue ... thinking lightly of the possession of gold and other property.' Self-controlled, moderate and sober they 'saw clearly that all these goods are increased by virtue and friendship with one another'.

The combination of the attractiveness of these Atlanteans and the minute details of the city's geography and daily life given in the story has made it irresistible to all kinds of people. For why, the argument goes, would Critias – or Plato for that matter – have invented all these irrelevant details if Atlantis was created out of his imagination, a metaphor for some ideal state? Why bother with the details of what fruits and crops were grown in this imaginary world? Why say of what colour stone the houses were made? Why describe the depths of the canals or the length of the road bridges? Why mention the strange detail of bath houses with hot and cold water? And bull worship?

Moreover, it is not as unlikely as it sounds to discover that Greek myths can have a basis in fact. The city of Troy only existed in Homer's stories – until the German banker and amateur archaeologist Heinrich Schliemann found the ruins of the real city of Troy in the late nineteenth century. Before Sir Arthur Evans found the ruined palace of Knossos on Crete, with its evidence of bull worship, people had assumed that the story of the minotaur was just a story. So why not Atlantis?

Archaeologists routinely scoff at the idea of Atlantis, but a new science called 'catastrophism' is lending weight to those who believe that in the past – and indeed in times to come – whole cultures can flourish and then simply be destroyed by some natural disaster.

Dale Dominey Howes explains: 'For a long time experts have considered that environmental processes take place at a uniform, regular, slow pace, and that change takes a long time to occur. But more recently a group of scientists called "catastrophists" have come to realise that actually the environment is not a continuously evolving slow thing, but is punctuated by hard hitting, high magnitude events that actually change the course of history.'

Dale Dominey Howes, a British volcanologist and disaster management expert, now at Macquarie University in Sydney, Australia is a self-confessed catastrophist. He is not remotely interested in the legend of Atlantis but he *does* believe that the geological record of our planet speaks of repeated natural catastrophes on a gigantic scale that have an enormous influence on both the environment and on human life and culture. Floods of quite staggering power that sweep away life and resculpt the landscape; super volcanoes that dump huge quantities of ash over a wide area, making cultivation impossible and altering the global weather for a time; impacts from space, meteorites and comets, that are capable of driving to extinction 90 per cent of life on earth – these are the truly awe-inspiring natural cataclysms that change life on a global scale.

But more local events – earthquakes, volcanoes, shifts in the patterns of local climate – can also change the course of history – and not just in the distant past. Dale points to the 1964 Alaska earthquake as a good recent example. This was an immensely powerful earthquake that shook nearly 800,000 square kilometres of this sparsely populated state for nearly three minutes. It lifted parts of the land so they ended up 38 metres higher than they had been before the earthquake. Other parts of Alaska were moved as much as 77 metres sideways. There were landslides and local tsunamis, and the very shape of the coastline changed. There was enormous damage to houses in Anchorage. Had such an earthquake taken place on another part of the volatile Pacific rim – near Seattle for example, or under Japan – then the death, destruction and economic damage would have been enormous.

If such a disaster hit Atlantis, then – according to the catastrophists – large parts of the island might have vanished, drowned by a mega-flood, or sunk by an earthquake, like the Alaskan one, a Magnitude 9. The whole civilisation *could* indeed have crumbled.

A cataclysmic event like this, in the distant past, would have had such an enormous physical and psychological effect on the people who lived through it that, as Dale Dominey Howes points out, it would definitely have been incorporated into myths and legends. He says: '(The people) didn't write down things ... that they'd experienced. What they would have done is told stories about it and they would have passed these stories from generation to generation through hundreds of years ... The types of event ... actually make it into folklore and mythology. They are the types of stories that are told time and time again. In fact, they're the stories of legend.'

So what could the disaster have been that sunk Atlantis? And where could the island state have been?

Critias told Socrates that Atlantis had flourished some 9,000 years before they were speaking, and this date coincides eerily with one of the greatest changes to the global environment that has happened in human times. 20,000 years ago, when the Ice Age still had Earth in its grip, the sea level was 120 to 130 metres lower than it is today. Vast quantities of water that are now in the oceans were then locked up in the ice caps. For this reason, the shape of the inhabitable world then was very different from its shape today. The Persian Gulf was dry, North America and Siberia were joined, Western India stretched far into the Indian

Ocean and southern India was joined to Sri Lanka, while south-east Asia was a vast dry continent about the size of North America. On all these lost lands there were, most likely, human beings living.

The warming of the Earth's climate has not been a gradual one, accompanied by the gentle melting of the ice and a slow rising of the seas. As far as can be told from the evidence, the sea rose in three dramatic flooding events: the first took place around 14,000 years ago, the second around 11,500 years ago and the third, and most dramatic, around 8,000 years ago. Though the sea would have risen by different amounts in different parts of the world, the last of these great floods would in some places – around the Atlantic for example – have led to a sea level rise of 40 centimetres in two days, and over the next 50 years a rise of 25 metres. In places where some local topographical barrier held back the waters for a time and then let them come flooding through – like the Black Sea and the western part of North America – the effect would have been sudden and apocalyptic. As so many of the sudden floods were the result of the shifting of enormous and heavy ice caps, the floods would also have been accompanied by earthquakes and tsunamis as the Earth's crust rebounded from the heavy weight.

Geneticist and author Dr Stephen Oppenheimer believes that these events explain the existence of flood myths – like Noah's Flood – in almost every culture, from almost every corner of the world. Could this natural disaster also have been the one that brought about the end of Atlantis? Geologists' understanding of what happened around the world 11,500, 9,000 and 5,500 years before Plato's time certainly strikes a chord with what he wrote about the ending of the lost island: 'Afterwards there occurred violent earthquakes and floods; and in a single day and night ... the island of Atlantis ... disappeared in the depths of the sea.'

But if this explains how a real Atlantis could have been lost, just as the story describes, does it help us discover where the ancient civilisation was located? Any one of the lands lost during these disastrous floods could hold the ruins of an Atlantis. Stephen Oppenheimer believes that the civilisation worst affected by the flooding at the end of the Ice Age was that part of the world that today has the greatest concentration and the greatest variety of flood myths: south-east Asia. The sea drowned a vast area of land that would have linked Malaysia, Borneo, what is now the South China Sea and all the islands of Indonesia into one large continent. Oppenheimer's work on linguistics, archaeology and genetics suggests that this area was at that time home to a relatively advanced culture. It was a society that traded long distances, had mastered the sea and had a developed agriculture. And it was dispersed or lost when the floods came.

Many people have told him that he has found Atlantis, and he admits that the evidence is persuasive. The drowned continent of south-east Asia would have been a large, flat plain ringed by impressive mountains – as Atlantis was said to be. Critias talks of there being two crops a year in Atlantis – possible in this tropical location – and he goes into great detail about the fertility of the soil and the irrigation canals, both of which are impressive features of the Indonesian islands of Java, Sumatra and Bali today. The ritual slaughter of bulls is practised in parts of Indonesia, just as Plato wrote that it was in Atlantis.

And there are more details in the Greek story that, as Oppenheimer points out, make sense if Atlantis were in south-east Asia: 'Elephants (are) very clearly described by Plato, and there's something which sounds very close to a coconut: a fruit with a hard rind with meat inside which you can make ointment out of to put on your face.'

But if this tale of a prosperous civilisation that vanished has its origin in south-east Asia and in the cataclysmic floods of 6000 BC, how could it have travelled so many thousands of miles to reach Egypt?

Trade between the East and Europe is in fact very old. There is definite evidence that a trade in spices existed by 200 BC. But recently a discovery at an archaeological site in Syria suggests that the trade may be much older. A pot of cloves dating back to 1700 BC has been found at a place called Turka. Cloves are only grown in two islands in the Moluccas in eastern Indonesia and so these must have travelled all that distance. Coconuts dating back to a similar time have also been found in Egypt and they too originate in the East. If a spice or a coconut can travel, surely a legend can travel too.

Though he believes that such stories would have travelled from East to West with traders and migrants, Oppenheimer does not believe this adds up to an 'Atlantis – found at last'. He says, 'There are a number of similarities, but I have to say that I don't buy this particular theory.'

Indeed, he thinks that one Atlantis never existed. He believes Plato's story is in fact a mixture of real historical elements remembered in the oral tradition of the eastern Mediterranean and combined to make a single story. The first is a story from the recent past – a historical conflict between the Ancient Greeks and some of their Mediterranean neighbours. The second is a distant folk memory of how the Mediterranean coastal communities were affected by the dramatic climate change and sea level rise that happened five and a half thousand years before Plato was writing. And the third element that he believes Plato wove into his story of an exotic lost land is the information that was beginning to creep into Greek society about the produce of other parts of the world with long distance trading. In his opinion, it is this third element in the Atlantis story that has created all the difficulties: 'The third story in the background in Plato's description of Atlantis is the one that's probably thrown everybody, because it talks about things that happen *outside* the

Mediterranean … Exotic animals such as elephants, exotic fruits such as coconuts, bull worship and two crops a year. All of these (are) suggestions of somewhere tropical and very lush … This may have nothing to do with the war that they were talking about. It may actually be a record of the end point of trade between tropical Asia, India or south-east Asia, and the Near East and the Mediterranean.'

But when Plato is so clear in his details, why suggest that his story is a muddled amalgam of different elements?

Jim Allen is an enthusiastic Atlantis-hunter who is impatient with those who do not consider that Plato's story could possibly be accurate. He came to the Atlantis mystery via a fascination with ancient measuring systems. Everything he has researched, read and studied about the ancient world – from the Aztecs to the Phoenicians, from the Egyptians to the Incas and the people who built Stonehenge – has convinced him of the extraordinary skills and knowledge of ancient peoples. Though he does not claim that every last sentence of Plato's two stories should be taken literally, he believes that the basic facts should be taken as they are written: 'The important point is that apart from all the other things Plato writes about Atlantis, underlying the story was a very detailed geographic description which applies to only one country or one place, and that place is today called South America. It's such a precise thing that we can't just throw it away on one side and say, "Well, it couldn't possibly be true", because ... they're such small details that fit only to this region that there must be some small truth behind this story.'

When he first started hunting for Atlantis, more than 20 years ago, he took as the starting point for his detective trail, the precise measurements given in the written account: that the capital city of Atlantis was in the middle of a large rectangular plain, 3,000 *stades* long and around 2,000 *stades* wide, and the geographical location was outside the Mediterranean. These pieces of information, Allen believes, are 'the key to the whole mystery'.

After years in the RAF, where he worked as a photographic interpreter, he is highly skilled in the interpretation of aerial maps and photographs. This unusual expertise he brought to bear on the hunt for Atlantis. He gathered together an enormous collection of maps and aerial photographs, and by measuring the size of known features on maps and on photographs of the same places he was able to cross-reference scales and so could always be sure of the exact size of the features he was analysing. Armed with this skill, and a scale drawing of the rectangular plain of Plato's story, he went hunting for the lost island. He explains, 'Plato says that Atlantis was a continent. It was as large as Libya and Asia together, and he says specifically that it was in the Atlantic Ocean opposite the pillars of Hercules, which means the Strait of Gibraltar. So I looked at America, that is to say all of America – North America, and South America – and I had a little scale drawing of a rectangular plain. I went north to south and looked for a place where this would fit in.'

It's a tedious and time-consuming job scouring the entire continent of America for a place that fits Plato's description. But, undiscouraged and with precision his watchword, Jim continued to search until he found a place that fitted the bill. It was on the west coast of South America, a high plateau to the south of Lake Titicaca in Bolivia, an area that is known as the altiplano. He observes, '(Plato) says it's enclosed by mountains, and a point people don't realise is that he says it's high above the level of the sea and the whole area rises precipitously out of the sea to a great height. This is what the altiplano is.'

Jim Allen is now sure that when Plato wrote about 'Atlantis' he meant the whole landmass of South America, and when he wrote about the citadel – the main city that ruled Atlantis – then he was referring to the Bolivian altiplano. This matched Plato's geographical description of the lost continent. But Jim Allen's research did not stop with aerial photographs. He immersed himself in books about the geography, the history, the folklore, the religion and the anthropology of South America. So many other details also slotted neatly into place: '(Plato) talks about things like the metals that existed there, such as gold, silver, copper, tin – which is actually a kind of a rare metal you don't find just anywhere in the world – and another mystery metal called orichalcum. Now even the translators of Plato's story had a problem with orichalcum. R G Berry says it might have been a mountain copper, and Sir Desmond Lee said it was probably an imaginary metal … But in fact in the Andes we have a metal (orichalcum) which is a natural alloy of gold and copper, and it's actually mined in Bolivia and other parts of the Andes, just like Plato said it was.'

Like all volcanic mountains, the Andes have hot springs as well as cold ones, just as Atlantis was said to have done. On the aerial photographs and satellite images of the altiplano Jim Allen found impressive linear features that he thought could be canals. He discovered that around Lake Titicaca there was evidence that the pre-Columbian peoples of the region had used irrigation canals to grow two crops a year. Jim Allen's research into pre-Conquistador South America has shown him that it is quite possible that the ancient peoples of South America cultivated a range of fruit and vegetables.

When he was eventually able to visit Bolivia, Jim Allen was struck by many more similarities between the altiplano and Atlantis. In the story, Critias tells how the God Poseidon created the island of Atlantis as three concentric circles of land, each ringed by water. Exploring the huge, dusty and inhospitable region today, scrambling up rocky outcrops and down into dried up ditches, Jim Allen found the three rings he was looking for: He says: 'That is exactly what we found. We climbed up an outer ring of land and beyond that there's a very wide gully which has got sand in the bottom. We climbed up this next mountain region. Beyond that there was another wide gully again with sand at the bottom. (The sand I think actually came from the earthquakes which destroyed the place.) And then we climbed the central mountain exactly as Plato describes it. We looked all round about, and all round about the place was this level smooth plain that Plato described, and just to the north running past this site was a kind of artificial canal.'

In the distance he could see the remains of what would once have been a large inland lake – the 'sea' that Plato wrote that the canal flowed into. He even found the red, white and black stones that the story told the city of Atlantis was built of.

Jim also made other connections. On Lake Titicaca, he found people living on floating islands. He speculates: 'So these are perhaps the original inhabitants of the area. They are water folk, and "water" in Aztec is *Atl*', so these are the "Atl" people. And the "Antis" part of the name in Quechua – the Inca language – means "copper". So what we call the Andes mountains are actually the Copper mountains ... And if I want to go a bit further into that line, the Inca name for the country of course wasn't America it was ... "the land of the four quarters". One of these quarters was called Antis ... Antisuyo, the kingdom of the Antis.'

But most amazing of all to him was the discovery of a local Bolivian folk tale: '(It) is a story of a city on the edge of a lake, and the story says that these people once upon a time were good people but they lost all the divine qualities. The gods walked among them and decided to punish them, and in one single day the gods punished the city and sank it in earthquakes and floods. Now here we have a Bolivian story which is exactly the same as Plato's story, so we must say to ourselves, I'm sure the Aymara Indians weren't reading Plato's book, so is it not possible that Plato's story came, as he said, from Egypt?'

Jim Allen believes the story reached Egypt from Atlanteans who travelled down the rivers of South America to the Atlantic coast, across the bottom of Africa, and up the Indian Ocean and the Persian Gulf on giant reed boats. There, he argues, they had contact with the Mesopotamians and Egyptians – they may even have founded those civilisations.

But this South American solution to the mysterious lost city does not fit quite so neatly in every particular. Clearly South America did not disappear into the Atlantic ocean leaving only a barrier of mud. Nor could the altiplano – which is at many thousands of metres – have vanished beneath the ocean waves.

'However, if you take the continent as being the whole of south America,' Jim Allen quickly explains, 'and the island that sank as being a volcanic island on the Altiplano, that is very, very possible to sink in the space of a single day and night, especially when we have these underground wells on the Altiplano that push all the water up from the ground. Now even on the expeditions that I've made there, what is a perfectly dry piece of ground one moment when it starts raining very quickly becomes a giant inland sea. The whole thing just floods.'

But the most serious objection to Jim Allen's thesis is the fact that no archaeology of an advanced but vanished civilisation pre-dating the Greeks has ever been found on the Bolivian altiplano. The evidence he cites – linguistic, artistic, documentary – is all relatively recent, most of it dating from times much nearer to our time than to Plato's.

Like so many of the candidates put forward for Atlantis, Bolivia requires a selective reading of Plato's story. It also exists in an archaeological vacuum, and requires the story to have reached Egypt and then Greece by a circuitous and complicated route. But there is a much more obvious place to search for the origin of the story of Atlantis: within the Mediterranean world that Plato would have known.

At the turn of the twentieth century, British archaeologist Sir Arthur Evans found the remains of an impressive civilisation on the Mediterranean island of Crete. He called it Minoan – after the Greek myth of the minotaur. Though previously no one had imagined that a European civilisation that predated the Greek and was contemporaneous with the early Egyptian could have existed, in the century since Evans first started excavating, numerous digs on Crete have helped to create a detailed picture of an impressive and powerful culture that flourished there from around 2200 BC to around 1400 BC.

Even now new evidence of the culture, power and influence of the Minoans is emerging every digging season. Dr Wolfgang-Dietrich Niemeier is Director of the German School of Archaeology in Athens. He has excavated Minoan sites not just on Crete, but all over the Eastern Mediterranean – on Cyprus, on the Turkish mainland, on Greek islands like Rhodes, and even in present-day Israel. The evidence he has unearthed has been remarkable and varied. On Rhodes he found cooking implements; in Israel, beautiful wall paintings with seascapes of boats, and decorative plants. Everywhere he found large quantities of pottery, and in northern Egypt evidence that Minoan craftsmen were so valued for their particular talents in home decorating that they were employed by wealthy clients far from Crete.

At that time Crete was a very wealthy and secure island. The great palaces for which the Minoans have become famous did not have fortifications: the leadership clearly felt they were unnecessary, fearing neither enemies nor pirates. Their boats – which used the new technology of sail – dominated the seas, and this, combined with Crete's geographical position, enabled the Minoans to become leaders in trade and business in the Eastern Mediterranean. In Niemeier's opinion, the Minoans operated a virtual monopoly on trade.

Of all the trading that Cretan merchants did, Niemeier's evidence suggests that the trading in metals was most crucial. This period is known to archaeologists as the Bronze Age, and it is clear from numerous finds of implements and weapons that bronze was highly valued by the Minoans. Bronze is manufactured by mixing 90 per cent copper with 10 per cent tin. The only place tin is known to have been found at that time is Afghanistan. It was brought from the mountains through Mesopotamia to Syria and eventually to a town where Minoan merchants lived. They bought the tin and sent it on to Minoan settlements around the Mediterranean. Like visitors to Atlantis, those visiting Crete at this time would have been impressed by the quantities of bronze in use among the Minoans.

Dr Colin MacDonald is also a Minoan specialist. Among this select group of experts, he has a particular distinction – one shared by very few archaeologists – for he found the first evidence of a writing system that had previously been unknown. In the Palace of Knossos, on Crete, he found a fragment of writing now called Linear A. It is a still undeciphered early Minoan writing system that has since been discovered at a number of other Minoan sites. Though no one knows what it says, the scrap of text is further evidence that here indeed was an advanced civilisation that – like

Atlantis – was literate. MacDonald calls it 'the first civilisation in Europe'.

More than a thousand years before the Ancient Greeks, the Minoans were a flourishing culture. Crete was a rich island providing grapes, olive oil, barley, wheat and all kinds of pulses for its population. Near the palace at Knossos were vast storehouses to hold food after harvest time. With trade came all kinds of knowledge of and contact with foreign countries, including those civilised centres in the Near East and Egypt. Rare and exotic items made it to Crete, like the elephant's tusks that have been excavated at the palace of Zakros in eastern Crete.

With its cosmopolitan trading network, its sea-going ships, its fertile and productive soil, its metal-working and its exotic items such as elephant tusks, Minoan Crete sounds tantalisingly like Atlantis. And there are other similarities, too. Colin MacDonald has been involved in the careful restoration of a group of four frescoes in the Knossos palace that show young men leaping over a bull. It is clear to him that bulls were an important part of religious activity among the Minoans, just as they were among the Atlanteans.

Colin MacDonald thinks there are good reasons for believing that if Plato based Atlantis on anything, it was on a civilisation in the Aegean. 'The Aegean is the earthquake centre of Europe and the Mediterranean. Earthquakes are very frequent in this area, and some of them are extremely catastrophic. Indeed, in Plato's time, in 373 BC, there was a massive earthquake which caused the town of Heliki to disappear. With that in mind, I think we can firmly place the myth of Atlantis in the Aegean area. In addition to that, the myth mentions Athens. And with Athens as a participant in the legend again, it's another reason for placing it in the Aegean area.'

But if Athens was truly able to be at war with this other civilisation, then the chronology given by Critias is dismissed by MacDonald in a sentence: 'The chronology set out in the myth of Atlantis is an impossibility. Dealing with a period so many thousands of years before Athens ever became great is just out of the question.'

Nine thousand years before Plato wrote, there was no advanced civilisation anywhere in Europe that corresponds to Plato's description, and archaeologists have found little evidence of anyone living on the Greek peninsula at that time at all. If Atlantis is based on something more than Plato's imagination, and it was at war with societies based on the Greek peninsula, then it must have existed no earlier than the second millenium BC.

If the civilisation of the Minoans was the model for Atlantis, did it fall apart as the story says, victim of a cataclysmic natural disaster?

The archaeological evidence suggests that Minoan power did wane, and that the civilisation that was recognisably Minoan did eventually vanish, to be replaced by other cultures and other rulers. But there seems little to suggest that this decline was rapid or sudden – nothing to justify a story of a whole island and a whole culture sinking in a day and a night beneath the waves.

Crete did suffer from earthquakes, but to Colin MacDonald's experienced eye, the damage they caused had a not wholly damaging effect on Cretan culture. He says: 'Earthquakes are relatively common in Crete, and even destructive earthquakes would have occurred once every 50 or 75 years. We see this reflected in the archaeological stratigraphy of the palace of Knossos, where an earthquake will destroy most of the palace and its surrounding buildings. And they seem to pick themselves up and build again, sometimes on an even grander scale. So an earthquake is not necessarily an event which causes a decline in civilisation. It can actually lead to greater things.'

But Minoan culture, as Dr Niemeier's work has shown, was not confined to Crete. And there is one place within the great Minoan empire where earthquakes were not the only danger.

In the 1960s a team of Greek archaeologists started to excavate on the island of Santorini, 110 kilometres north of Crete. Once known as the 'round' island, Santorini is now not one but five fragments of islands, grouped around an irregular oval stretch of sea. This stretch of sea is in fact the crater of an enormous explosive volcano that has erupted on a number of occasions in recorded history. The island is covered in layers of ash, pumice and lava deposited by the volcano.

At a place called Akrotiri, the archaeologists began to dig down through many metres of ash searching for evidence of the communities that may have existed on Santorini in prehistoric times – communities that could have been buried by an eruption. And they struck lucky. Little by little their excavations began to reveal an Aegean Pompeii – a prosperous and bustling trading port preserved for ever at the moment when enormous quantities of ash fell from what must have been a gigantic eruption. From everything the archaeologists found (including some sesame seeds that could be carbon-dated), it was clear that this had been a Minoan trading port dating from the first half of the second millenium BC (2000-1500 BC).

Akrotiri was a town of two- and three-storey buildings, made of stone with wooden staircases. Though its inhabitants lived 4,000 years ago, it is clear from the evidence that they lived lives that would have impressed their contemporaries around the Mediterranean. In many ways, they seem quite familiar even today. On the ground floor there were workshops and store rooms. Grindstones for grinding corn and lead weights for weighing incoming produce have also been found there. They had cooking utensils and knives made of bronze. On the upper floors were living areas, and evidence was found that weaving was commonly done here. These upstairs rooms often had large windows to let in the light, and the walls were decorated with lively paintings. There was even mains drainage.

Many of the floors were simply beaten earth, but others were made of crushed seashells or stone slabs. Like the port Critias describes in Atlantis, Akrotiri was a busy place, with houses crammed together, connected by winding lanes and passageways. It must have been noisy too. In many of the houses there were found beautiful pottery vases, jugs and storage jars, decorated with elegant swirling patterns and graceful swallows, fat barley heads and palm trees. There were dolphins pictured, too.

The people of Akrotiri lived well. There is evidence that the fertile volcanic soil and their extensive trading network brought them as wide a range of produce as the Atlanteans were said to enjoy. They ate barley and pulses; they had wine, olive oil and sesame seeds; they grew the fragrant herbs, thyme and saffron (which is extracted from crocuses). The bones found in rubbish tips suggest they ate pork and goat, fish and shellfish.

Though these city walls were not covered in gold, tin and bronze, as Critias says of Atlantis, the interior walls of the houses were decorated with wonderful paintings. And these too give away secrets about the long-lost Minoans. One shows a pair of monkeys scrambling on a rock. Zoologists have identified them as a species that comes from Ethiopia. Had the painter travelled to Africa? Or had the monkeys been brought to the Aegean on a sailor's shoulder? Two young boys with long black hair box naked while two other young men carry bunches of grey-blue fish. There are women with gold jewellery and heavy make-up. One frieze shows boats with sails and oars, four-square houses in tightly packed towns, dolphins and deer, and men in white robes.

It is not just the wall painting with its graceful boats that suggests the people of Akrotiri had a confident command of the sea. Plenty of evidence has been found in the houses of trade with Egypt (ostrich egg shells and stone vases); with Syria (amphorae), with the Near East (metals) and with Crete (pottery). And only a fraction of the settlements that must have been on Santorini before the eruption have been excavated.

Though it was clearly nothing like the large size attributed to Atlantis nor in the correct geographical location, already Santorini is beginning to sound similar to the famous lost city. Houses on the island were built – like those of Atlantis – of red, white and black volcanic rock. There are hot and cold springs on the island and perhaps – as at Knossos and in Plato's story – they were harnessed to provide hot baths.

But the greatest similarity to the story and the biggest clue that this really is the most likely origin of the myth is the way this prosperous life was brought to a sudden end: when the volcano rumbled to life. It was a powerful eruption – indeed one of the most powerful volcanic eruptions on earth in the past 10,000 years. Before the eruption Santorini volcano rose 300 metres above sea level. When the volcano became calm once more, there was nothing left of that volcanic cone – just a hole in the sea 200 metres deep, and for any surviving people of the island a shattered world.

So if the Minoan settlement on Santorini and its violent destruction was the germ of truth behind Plato's story of Atlantis, can we establish the date it disappeared?

The evidence of the archaeological digs suggests that life in Akrotiri came to its sudden end some time around 1500 BC. In the 1980s, an American study of the tree rings on Californian bristlecone pines suggested a date of 1627 BC. There is evidence of frost damage in the tree rings of bristlecones for that year, and this is usually associated with volcanic eruptions. They can throw such large quantities of ash and sulphuric acid into the upper atmosphere that global temperatures are significantly lowered and so affect the growing rates of trees right around the world. Mike Baillie is a dendrochronologist at Queen's University, Belfast. He studies the tree rings of Irish bog oaks. He says: 'When we went and looked at our trees, lo and behold, we discovered that there is a growth down-turn – really severe growth down-turn – which starts in 1628 and runs on for several years through the 1620s BC. And it turns out that that's also seen in other records. We certainly see it in England, we see it in

Germany and it's probably there in Scandinavia and also in Anatolia.'

The difference in one year is easily explained by the time it would have taken for the ash to travel from the Aegean to create weather problems in the mountains of California. But tree rings are not the only record of past weather that the experts can read. 'Once you've got used to the idea of tree rings being a year by year record,' explains Mike Baillie, 'the next most equivalent record that science has is the record of compressed snowfall in Greenland. It's a really remarkably simple thing. Greenland is so cold that when the snow falls one year, it simply lies, and the next year the snow falls on top, and it just does this every year. Hence it builds up over something like the last 150,000 years about 3 kilometres depth of ice. And it is the compressed annual snowfall.'

Ice cores have been drilled through this accumulation of thousands of years of snow, and experts can analyse it to tell what the weather was doing at certain times in the earth's past. Some claim that for the upper part of the record they can actually see the individual layers of annual snowfall for something like 40,000 years. When there are layers of sulphuric acid in the ice core, then they know that a big volcano erupted somewhere on earth. Mike Baillie is duly impressed: 'I mean this is astonishing stuff. They can work their way down from the top, just like tree rings working their way back. The only snag is they can't check the results as well as we can because we've got lots of trees and they've got very few ice cores.'

The result is that ice core dates can be out by about 1 per cent – in other words, by about 10 years every millennium. In one ice core, researchers looking for evidence of the date of the Santorini eruption found a layer of acid that came out with a date of 1645 BC, and a second core yielded a layer dated at 1636 BC. Given the slight inaccuracy of ice core dates, Mike Baillie is convinced that the tree ring date of 1628 BC is the actual date the Santorini volcano blew.

How close can we come to understanding what happened in the last hours of the real Atlantis?

The answer is, very close. Thanks to detailed work done by volcanologists on the layers of ash, pumice and rock on the island of Santorini, and on the ash and pumice that can still be found today around the eastern Mediterranean, it is possible to reconstruct the last days and hours of life on the island.

It began with a series of earthquakes. At Akrotiri – and doubtless at other towns, now completely lost to history – terrified people must have fled from their houses into the countryside as the stone buildings rocked. Then, when the shocks appeared to have come to an end (and earthquakes were not unknown to the people of Santorini), they must have returned to their homes. Excavating the buried town, archaeologists have found evidence that people had begun to clear rubble from the streets. Workmen had even started to repair the damage. But earthquakes, it soon turned out, were only a precursor of what was to come.

Today, on the inside wall of the volcano's crater where it emerges from the sea, there is an extraordinary sight to be seen. Volcanic ash, laid down in layers, each one slightly different, provides a minute by minute record of what the volcano did all those centuries ago.

Volcanologist Dale Dominey Howes has studied the Santorini volcano and can now read these layers like a book. And he can tell the story of the volcano like a novel. At the base of the cliff he locates a brownish layer that in Minoan times was the top layer of soil. This was the earth the people cultivated and walked upon. Immediately above this layer is one of ash, which suggests there was some precursory activity – that the volcano must have puffed a little ash for a time before the cataclysmic eruption.

Then comes the layer that tells the story of Day One. Dominey Howes says: 'This part of the eruption was effectively dry. No water was getting into the exploding volcano. The eruption column is blowing up into the sky maybe 36-38 kilometres above our heads. And the pumice and the ash is starting to rain down around us. This part of the eruption probably lasted about one day and at the maximum intensity the ash and the pumice were raining down and accumulating at a rate of around 3 and 5 centimetres per minute, which is incredibly fast.'

For the people of Akrotiri and the other towns and villages on Santorini, it must have been terrifying. The high ash column would have blocked out the sun, making it dark even in the day time. Ash and small pieces of pumice would have been raining down from the sky, hitting people on the head as they ran to take shelter; accumulating in heavy layers on roofs until they collapsed; making it difficult to even walk, let alone run, and almost impossible to breathe. Old people, children, animals would all have been choking in the dense ashy darkness.

No bodies have been found at Akrotiri, nor have any of the kinds of precious jewellery that is shown on the wall paintings. It seems this first day of the eruption was sufficiently terrifying to trigger an organised evacuation of the town. Families must have gathered up their most precious possessions and hurried to the dockside. Perhaps there were enough trading vessels, fishing boats and warships in port to load all the citizens on in an orderly fashion. Then sails would have been raised and oars plunged into the sea, and the men would have rowed the boats away in the choking darkness, heading for safety.

More likely, though, as Colin MacDonald suggests, were we able to see what still lies beneath the ash or beneath the waters of the vast caldera, we would find (as they have near Pompeii) the tragic remains of people huddled together at the shore, waiting desperately for some means of escape. But in vain, for the terrifying first phase of the eruption, with its massive column filling the sky and visible all the way to Crete and even Egypt, was to be followed by something even worse.

The cone of the volcano was on a small island out to sea. As the violent eruption continued to shake the mountain, sea water was able to come into contact with the red hot magma – with disastrous consequences. 'During the second phase of the eruption – that starts about here,' says Dominey Howes, pointing to the next layer in the cliffside, 'the dynamics of the eruption have changed completely. Water has started to get into the exploding vent, so the intensity, the power, the energy, has increased quite a lot. Now, in this part of the eruption sequence it gets much more explosive. There are big bangs, big explosions, much more material is being blown out of the vent, and this material is starting to roll down the side of the volcano and across the land surface.'

Pyroclastic flows now cascaded down the volcano's flanks. These glowing clouds of ash, dust, rock and gas are heavier than air and cling to the ground. Rushing down the mountainside at high speed and at a temperature of 200–300 degrees centigrade, they would have incinerated and blown to pieces anything in their path.

A change in the colour of the cliff face tells of the next phase in the deadly eruption. Says Dominey Howes: 'Where this line of black rocks is ... is where the whole sequence has changed in style again ... Parts of the side of the old volcano are falling down into the vent and then being exploded out like missiles and projectiles, which are flying through the air again – 100-200 miles [160-320kph] an hour.'

Akrotiri town was around 10 kilometres from the crater of the volcano and yet some of these missiles – known as volcanic bombs – crashed onto the town itself.

Now at last the eruption came to an end. But the island of Santorini was a completely different place. According to Dominey Howes, 'Over in the north-western areas, parts of the caldera wall had collapsed into the sea, opening a whole new channel to the north-west. Out to the east of the island so much material had been deposited onto the land that the coastline had migrated two kilometres in an easterly direction. Places that used to be islands were now joined to the main island, so the whole of the landscape looked completely different.'

This was not the only change. Ash now blanketed the entire island.

It would have looked like a lunar landscape, grey and desolate, with no animals, no plants, no towns, no farms, no people. For all practical purposes, the island had vanished, just like the Atlantis of legend.

Huge rafts of pumice that had been ejected by the volcano, and which float because they are so full of air, washed around the Mediterranean, presenting a hazard to shipping. Was it the memory of this that

Plato records as the strange aftermath of the disappearance of Atlantis – that it left an impassable barrier of mud to mark where it had once been?

Though Santorini would have been uninhabitable for many years, Minoan culture itself did not disappear instantly. However, as tree-ring data from around Europe shows, Santorini was not the only place affected by the blast. Ash that can be traced to the volcano has been found all around the eastern Mediterranean. The eruption also sparked off tsunamis – tidal waves – that would have crashed ashore and flooded coastal areas around the eastern Mediterranean.

As Dale Dominey Howes says, the effects of the eruption right across the Aegean would have been great: 'You actually only need a very light fall of ash to cause burning and destruction of crops … We think that over a period of several years afterwards the ash falls poisoned the soil (and) made it difficult to grow crops. As a consequence, people would have starved … and that would have led to other diseases breaking out in the population.'

Those who had been nearer to the volcano would have suffered the long-term health consequences of breathing in volcanic ash, and there would have been widespread economic problems caused by crop failures and a sudden influx of refugees.

From the fragments of information in the archaeological record, Colin MacDonald has pieced together the effects of the eruption on the island of Crete, the heart of Minoan power and culture. Before 1628 BC the Minoan civilisation was at its peak, with power based on the great palaces. After the eruption, there seems to have been a political disintegration on the island, with smaller settlements beginning to take more control over their own areas and less homage being paid to the palaces like Knossos. He has also found a new style of pottery that, with its motifs of sea life, especially on ritual vessels, he thinks may reflect a greater awareness of the sea in the wake of the tsunamis that the volcano would have created. Did the gigantic and destructive waves, appearing suddenly from the open sea, never breaking but rushing ever inland, do memorable damage to boats and coastal communities?

But these practical problems would perhaps have been dwarfed by the psychological effects of witnessing such a sudden and cataclysmic natural event that people could neither control nor understand. Says MacDonald, 'They probably wouldn't have trusted the earth any more – everything that they'd known would have changed. What was going to happen in the future? Could this type of thing occur again? It really would have had a big effect on their psyche.'

MacDonald has found evidence of a grisly kind that hints at some kind of crisis of faith in existing religious leaders and practices. Desperate measures seem to have been adopted in a ritual attempt to cope with the disasters that had struck them: human sacrifice and cannibalism. At one site, he found four or five young people had been killed, their bodies butchered and the meat sliced off the bone, all in a religious context.

But why is there no written record of this extraordinary natural event that had such a damaging effect on Minoan civilisation? Like the Atlanteans, the Minoans possessed writing but, curiously enough – as far as anyone knows – writing was only used for record-keeping and not for literature or history. So there is no Minoan account of the end of Santorini and the slow disintegration of the Minoan civilisation that had dominated so much of the eastern Mediterranean for over 500 years.

So is Santorini Atlantis? Archaeologist Wolf-Dietrich Niemeier laughs nervously. He believes that historians and archaeologists can and should use myths and stories as evidence in their attempt to understand the past, but he cautions that they must be very careful in how they interpret them: 'The myth of Atlantis ... is a very controversial theme. I think mostly it is really an *idea* of Plato's. I don't believe that there ever was a real Atlantis. But of course Plato may reflect traditions about Minoan Crete in this. He is constructing an ideal society and a kind of golden age and ... we often find the Minoan civilisation reflected in (this) myth of a golden age.'

It seems plain to Colin MacDonald, too, that such a disaster must have burned itself into the minds of the people who lived through it: 'It's almost impossible to believe that such a thing would not have stayed in the minds of the Minoans and have been passed down orally through the centuries.'

The story would have entered into the folklore of communities right around the Mediterranean, wherever travellers met and exchanged news and stories. Some details would have stuck in people's memories; others would have been embellished and improved with the telling; others would have been forgotten. It isn't surprising that the location of the vanished island, of the golden culture, should over the centuries have migrated westwards to the great Atlantic Ocean beyond the Pillars of Hercules. This was the place of the setting sun, where Homer sited Elysium, the land of the blessed dead. Where better to place a wealthy and cultured civilisation, lost in the mists of time but representing in its way a vanished golden age.

CHAPTER 6

The Mystery of the Bermuda Triangle

There are places in the oceans of the world where strange things are said to happen. Those who have sailed there talk of navigation equipment and radios that malfunction; others claim that time itself stands still. Boats both small and large, and even aeroplanes simply disappear without trace.

In the Pacific it happens in an area the Japanese know as the Devil's Sea; in Central Asia, it happens in the huge land-locked Caspian Sea; and, most famously of all, it happens in the Bermuda Triangle.

But are these stories of vanishing boats and aeroplanes just travellers' tales – a legend built on hype, on scientific ignorance and a gullible public?

Now one British scientist has found intriguing evidence that a genuine natural phenomenon may be at the root of these stories. If he's right, travelling by sea may be an even more dangerous activity than people believe ...

In November 2000 a hi-tech survey vessel usually under contract to the international oil industry set sail from Aberdeen heading north-east out into the North Sea. On board was oceanographer Professor Alan Judd from Sunderland University and Dr Robert Prescott, a marine archaeologist and specialist in Scottish fishing boats, from the Scottish Institute of Marine Studies at St Andrew's University. Their destination was an area of the North Sea known to generations of British fishermen as the Witches' Ground (the name refers to a fish known as a witch that makes up a significant proportion of the catch in this part of the North Sea). It would take them 12 hours through swelling seas to reach it. Once there, Alan Judd hoped to find evidence for a theory he has been developing over many years.

Alan Judd is a modest and cautious man. As a professor in the Geology department at Sunderland University, he is in demand as a consultant to the oil industry. He's an unlikely man to have found himself attracted to a subject as 'unscientific' as the Bermuda Triangle. But Judd's particular expertise is in the gas methane, and over the years, as his research and that of others has revealed more and more about the behaviour and extent of this gas in the world's oceans, his conviction has grown that methane may have been responsible for many of the most mysterious maritime disasters of the past.

The hundreds of stories of strange disappearances in that area of the Atlantic Ocean known as the Bermuda

Triangle go back more than a century. It is even said that Lloyds of London, the ship insurers, considered this area particularly dangerous from the time the Stuarts were on the throne of England. Christopher Columbus, too, is said to have reported strange things in this part of the Atlantic: weird white streaks in the ocean such as he had never seen elsewhere.

A tale from 1881 is typical of those that are told about the Bermuda Triangle. A ship named the *Ellen Austin* came upon a boat with a cargo of lumber, drifting there unmanned. There was no sign of any crew, so the skipper of the *Ellen Austin* detailed some of his men to take over the job of sailing the abandoned ship to the nearest port. They boarded the ghost ship and sailed away. But a few days later, she was found again. Drifting, unmanned again. There was no sign at all of the sailors from the *Ellen Austin*. For the second time, a new crew took her over. And that was the last anyone saw of the sailors – or ship. Both vanished without trace.

Or there's a story from 1921 with echoes of the *Marie Celeste*. The *Carroll A Deering* was apparently found stranded off Cape Hatteras, that most dangerous stretch of North Carolina coast, known to sailors as the 'graveyard of the Atlantic'. Though there was no sign of crew and no distress message had been received, when rescuers went on board they found tables set with food, half eaten; bunks made; lights on; food bubbling on the stove. Yet there was not a single crew member to be found, either dead or alive. Then, as night fell, reported residents living on the nearby islands, came the sounds of screams from the abandoned ship.

Most famous of all the Bermuda Triangle stories, perhaps, is the strange disappearance of five military training aircraft, known as Flight 19 in December 1944. The trainee air crew and their instructor set out together from Fort Lauderdale, north of Miami, Florida at 14.10 on what was to have been a two-hour training flight – and were never seen again. The weather had deteriorated rapidly during the flight and it seems likely, from the fragmentary radio messages that other planes in the vicinity were able to pick up, that the trainee pilots had got lost and had then run out of petrol as they flew in the wrong direction.

However, the disappearance of Flight 19 quickly became the focus of numerous stories. It was said that radio messages were received from the ill-fated aircraft to say that their instruments were malfunctioning. A plane sent up to search for them also disappeared without sending a distress signal, which deepened the sense of mystery. Rumours quickly circulated that, contrary to early reports, the weather had been fine and clear, and that other radio messages from the crew said the ocean looked strange, like 'white water' and that they no longer knew which direction was which. Soon the story was being told that the ill-fated crew had sent a desperate message warning people not to come after them to attempt a rescue.

Other stories from the Bermuda Triangle stress this supernatural element. They tell of time speeding up or slowing down; of an impenetrable yellow mist that envelops both boats and planes and causes crewmen to become so full of static electricity that their hair stands on end; of a gigantic whirlpool that sucks boats to their doom. Atlantis enthusiasts have suggested that a giant crystal that once provided power for the lost continent is at the bottom of the sea here and is the source of instruments going wrong and boats and planes sinking.

Such spooky goings-on as these are hard to credit and must owe more to the imagination than to any unseen hazard. But it's the stories of boats that disappear abruptly that interest Alan Judd. And boats of all sizes do disappear for no apparent reason from the triangle of ocean bounded by Bermuda in the north, and Miami and Cuba in the south-west and south-east respectively. A 300 metre coal ship called *Cyclops* disappeared with her crew of 309 in 1918. No wreckage or bodies were ever found. In 1958 millionaire yachtsman Harvey Conover and his family disappeared on their yacht. Again, no wreckage or bodies were ever found.

On average around 350 ships, larger than small pleasure yachts, disappear each year on the high seas. Of these, a handful vanish without giving a distress message of any kind, and not all are in the Bermuda Triangle. There are many reasons why a ship may sink, and the large number of boats, large and small, that go missing in this area of the Atlantic may be just a statistical coincidence. It is one of the busiest shipping areas of the world with a particularly high number of pleasure boats of all shapes and kinds. It is also an area with a high number of natural hazards.

One such hazard is a terrifying marine phenomenon called a 'rogue wave'. Like the Bermuda Triangle, stories of rogue or freak waves were dismissed as tall tales for hundreds of years before they were proved in the late twentieth century to be an actual fact. It was only when ships became big enough and strong enough to survive being hit by one of these monsters that it was realised they truly did exist. Now that they are a recognised phenomenon and ships' captains are encouraged to report sightings, eye-witness accounts of waves so high that they appear on the ship's radar as if they were land and that stop aircraft carriers dead in their tracks as if they had hit a brick wall are beginning to be told openly.

A gigantic abnormal wave can be caused when two sets of waves momentarily get in step, causing both the wave's height and its trough to be doubled. Such waves can be up to 30 metres high and 30 metres deep. The weight of water is enormous, and when it comes crashing down on the deck it can wrench steel like tin foil, tear off hatch covers, snap masts and smash portholes. Sometimes the weight of water itself just overwhelms the ship, and in this case it is sent plunging to the depths of the ocean without time for a Mayday of any kind.

Though commonest in those areas of the ocean where the continental shelf ends and the deep ocean begins – places like the Bay of Biscay – rogue waves are found across the world. Including in the Bermuda Triangle.

On Sunday 11 June 1984 a 35-metre square rigger called the *Marques* was sailing just north of Bermuda. She was a magnificent three-masted tall ship, one of nearly 40 such boats taking part in the regular transatlantic tall ships race. On board were 28 crew members, most of them young people. It was just before dawn and the majority of the crew were asleep below decks. There was heavy rain and the wind was beginning to get up, too. A 22-year-old American named Philip Sefton was at the helm of the ship.

All of a sudden there was a particularly strong gust of wind and the whole boat was pushed right down on the starboard side. Before she had had time to recover, Sefton was appalled to see a gigantic wave of freakishly large size bearing down on them. It slammed into the *Marques* with extraordinary force. The wave pushed the ship's masts beneath waves and in moments she was swamped. In less than a minute, the *Marques* had sunk. Philip Sefton and eight of his shipmates survived to be rescued. The remaining 19 died.

This part of the Atlantic is notorious for its tropical storms and hurricanes, and these can generate rogue waves. In a hurricane winds of more than 120 miles an hour are common and any ship caught up in such a storm could sink. But if a boat disappears in the Bermuda Triangle today during a tropical storm or a hurricane, no one would genuinely believe something inexplicable was at work. And weather satellites can pinpoint the location of even short-lived storms.

A new theory suggests that this part of the Atlantic may also be the home of even more extreme storms, called hypercanes. No one has ever witnessed such a storm but the theory goes that if a patch of the ocean heated up to over 104°F then an extremely compact and intense hurricane could be created. It might be as much as 30 kilometres high, with winds of 800 kilometres per hour. And it would die as quickly as it formed, once the storm moved away from such a patch of extremely hot sea. Meteorite impact or underwater volcanic activity have been suggested as possible mechanisms by which the sea could overheat in this way. Could such storms actually have happened and have sunk ships in the Bermuda Triangle?

Professor Alan Judd has another idea, one which has little to do with stormy weather and – if true – would not be a hazard confined to the Bermuda Triangle. He believes that spontaneous releases of methane gas from the bottom of the ocean could be responsible for the sudden and catastrophic sinking of ships.

Methane is a natural gas that is in fact the simplest hydrocarbon. It is a by-product of organic decay and so is present in many different environments. It leaks from land-fill sites and from paddy fields. It is also produced in large quantities by flatulent cattle. In some parts of the world – most spectacularly in the central Asian state of Azerbaijan, known for good reason as 'the land of fire' – it fuels the permanent flames that burn on some hillsides. But most interesting to Alan Judd is the methane that gathers at the bottom of the sea. Organic matter falls to the seabed and then gets buried beneath layers of sediment. Over time, the organic material is buried at a depth of 2 or 3 kilometres, and here the pressure and heat that are exerted make the organic material break down. Petroleum liquids and gasses, methane among them, are formed. Methane is a very short molecule chain. Because of this it is very buoyant and so migrates up through the layers of sediment towards the seabed. If the sediments are coarse-grained it can find its way to the surface relatively easily and so will seep out into the sea. But if the sediments are very fine-grained then the methane can find itself trapped at depth, in a pocket of gas with the pressure gradually accumulating over time.

Methane can also get trapped in a curious form called a gas hydrate. Gas hydrates are ice-like solid substances made of methane and water that exist where the sea water temperature is cold enough. They exist at shallow depths in the polar regions and under the permafrost. They even exist in tropical waters where the ocean is very deep, the pressure in its depths is very great and the temperature is extremely cold. Experts believe these hydrates may contain as much carbon as all the currently known deposits of natural gas and oil in the world put together. Finding out where hydrates are and how much methane they contain, however, is extremely difficult. Thus far, surveys have found large quantities on the continental margins right round the world: off the west and east coasts of North America, between Britain and Norway, off the coast of India and under the Caspian Sea. And experts predict that the methane hydrates they have found so far are only the tip, as it were, of the iceberg. There are certainly plenty in the Bermuda Triangle.

There are sea-faring tales from the past that describe the wild bubbling of the seas for no apparent reason. Joseph Conrad once wrote of such a sight. Geologists now believe these are caused by spontaneous releases of methane gas. Methane gas does not just escape from the seabed by gentle seepage. Extensive seabed surveys have shown that many are dotted with craters, known to geologists as pock marks. In the North Sea, for instance, pock marks cover 100,000 square kilometres of the sea floor. Most are 30 or 40 metres across and a few metres deep. But others are gigantic. One single pock mark in the North Sea has approximately the same volume as a football stadium. As Alan Judd says, 'If you were to try and dig that out with a JCB it would take you a year. And this

... seems to have been formed 13,000 years ago, in a single gas escape event.'

Gas comes rushing out into the water and thrusts the seabed sediment up in a cloud. Currents wash the finer grains away, and the coarser sediment then settles back down into the crater that is left.

But what causes the gas to rush out? Pressure building up under the seabed until it reaches breaking point, earthquake activity and even a change in barometric pressure in stormy weather are all possible causes of gas release.

A team of scientists from the US Naval Research Laboratory in Washington DC recently added another cause to this list: asteroid impact. They have found evidence to suggest that when the giant asteroid or comet plunged into what is now the Yucatan peninsula 65 million years ago the impact caused the release of enormous quantities of methane into the atmosphere. Lightning would have ignited the gas, causing a global fire storm that would have contributed to the disappearance of the dinosaurs. They also believe a smaller gas blow-out occurred in the Gulf of Mexico during the late Pleistocene era.

Just how much gas is released and with what consequences is now a matter of intensive scientific research. In Norway geologists are studying a catastrophic sub-marine landslide, known as the Storegga Slide, that took place around 7,000 years ago. Several hundred cubic kilometres of material were set in motion and created a tsunami that crossed the North Sea and would have devastated coastal Neolithic communities on the east coast of Britain. Gas hydrate experts believe the release of methane from gas hydrates played a part in making this event so damaging.

When methane is released it does not just affect the seabed. It also affects a fundamental property of sea water: its ability to hold up an object like a boat and enable it to float. If a large amount of gas gets into water, objects no long bob about in it buoyantly. A ship will sink like a stone. A man in a flotation suit will drop to his death unable to swim.

Workers in the oil industry are very familiar with what happens when gas escapes. If a rig drilling for oil hits a pocket of gas, an explosion is not the only danger. As gas fills the water column, the rig may lose its buoyancy and sink. Though no one in the oil industry likes to talk about it, drilling rigs have been lost this way. Some have been lost without a trace.

So could this account for the loss without trace of ships in the Bermuda Triangle? Are there large quantities of methane in that part of the Atlantic? Alan Judd puts it like this: 'A lot of people talk about the Bermuda Triangle and say, "Is this related to gas?" In that situation the temperature … at the seabed (is) actually cold enough and (there are) high enough pressures to form gas hydrates. The seabed is very unstable … So if for any reason – perhaps earthquake activity –

the seabed were to slump, then the temperature and pressure conditions might be changed such that the gas hydrate may decompose and a large volume of gas will suddenly be put into the water column. In that kind of situation, that gas is going to go straight through the water, and anything, any shipping, that happens to be there will inevitably sink and be lost without trace.'

It's a theoretical possibility. Perhaps methane was the cause of the white streaks in the sea that Columbus talked about. Judd believes the Bermuda Triangle, because of its unstable geology and the presence of gas hydrates, is one of the most likely places for this to occur. But thus far there is no concrete evidence of it happening.

The North Sea has clear evidence of gas escapes, some of them, judging by the size of the pock marks they formed, big enough to have involved large quantities of methane. But there is no tradition of ships sinking without reason in the North Sea the way there is in the Bermuda Triangle, so is the theory – that escaping methane could cause a ship to sink – no more than that: a neat theory?

In 1987 Alan Judd came across something rather strange that had the capacity to put some flesh on the bones of the theory. Since the early 1970s surveying ships for the oil industry had been finding evidence of pock marks on the seabed in the area of the North Sea known as the Witch Ground. Side scan sonar surveys discovered a particularly large pock mark – 120 metres from north to south, 90 metres from east to west and 3 metres in depth – that was named the Witch's Hole.

In the centre of the Hole, the sonar picked up a target. It looked as if it was a plume of escaping gas. At that time – in the mid-1970s – little work had been done on pock marks and there was a dispute going on as to what actually caused them. Some geologists suggested that they had nothing to do with gas and Alan Judd was keen to find out more about this gas plume. In 1987 he got his chance, when a further survey of the Witch's Hole was undertaken. He did not go out on the survey vessel himself but gave clear instructions for what he wanted: 'I asked the operators to do a survey close to the seabed so that we could get a good angle to have a look at the gas in detail. What, I didn't expect – or what they didn't expect – was that when the sonar towfish actually went through the pock mark it would hit something hard. We expected it to just pass through a bubble plume, but it hit something – an obstruction on the seabed.'

The results of the 1987 survey were an important part of settling the argument, demonstrating clearly that pock marks *were* caused by escaping gas. But it was the other discovery of the survey ship – this obstruction on the seabed – that proved for Alan Judd to be the more unexpected and ultimately the more intriguing.

For, recovering their sonar towfish, the survey engineers did a second trawl past the obstacle and this time they were able to obtain clear images. To the untrained eye, the streaks and blobs of a sonar image are hard to interpret, but to Alan Judd they are crystal clear: these particular lines were obviously a ship-wreck. He was able to measure the length and the breadth of the boat. The image was striped – 'rather like zebra stripes or pyjama stripes'. With the aid of a magnifying glass, he was able to actually count the individual stripes and in that way get an idea of the spacing of the structure of the ship. Seeking advice from a colleague who knew about ship-building, he was able to deduce that what he was seeing was the wooden framework of a ship from which the planks had fallen away. Detective work revealed that had the nails been copper they would not have rusted so the boat must have been constructed with steel nails. Judd says: 'So the conclusion we came to was that it was a Zulu-class wooden-hulled fishing boat which was built on the north-east coast of Scotland during the late 19th and early 20th century.'

But to Alan Judd the type of fishing boat was much less important than the possible reason why it came to be lying on the sea bed right in the middle of a pock mark: 'So the question is, how did it get there? Is it just pure happenstance? Or is there some causative feature, something about the pock mark which caused it to be there?'

In November 2000 he got the chance to take a closer

look. He was to travel out to the Witch Ground for the first time. This time he was on board a state-of-the-art surveying vessel with not just sonar but also a remotely operated vehicle (ROV) that would be able to descend to the wreck and take video images of it and the seabed on which it lay.

Dr Robert Prescott is an expert on the history of the Scottish fishing industry and he joined the survey with alacrity when he heard about the Zulu. He has a particular interest in this rare wooden fishing vessel and has even been involved in the restoration of one for the Scottish Fisheries Museum.

For 12 hours they sailed out into the North Sea, towards the north-east corner of the Forties oil field. It was a rough journey, but at last they reached the area where the Witch's Hole was to be found. Then started an anxious period as – hour after hour – the survey ship trawled the area searching for first the pock mark and then, when that was found, for the ship itself. The coordinates from the 1987 survey had been sketchy. To and fro they went and they found nothing. There was hardly a metre of the pock mark left to survey. Alan Judd was about to despair. Then they found it. For him it was a spectacular moment.

'We had a long period when we thought we knew where the wreck was. Then we surveyed round it and didn't see anything. The pressure on me, I felt, was getting greater and greater because everybody's here because I say there's a wreck here. Then we did what was going to be almost one of the last surveys and we hit a sonar target which was really completely different from anything else we'd seen. We had seen that we had a feature, the pock mark was there, but we hadn't seen the wreck until this last east-west traverse.'

Then they completed a further scan and saw that the outline of the wreck almost exactly matched the image from the 1987 survey. The shape, the length, the breadth, the characteristic striping were just as Alan had seen previously.

Now it was the moment to lower the ROV 150 metres to the bottom of the sea. Pictures from the ROV's video cameras were sent back to the screens on board the survey ship. Slowly it tracked across the featureless grey-brown seabed and then suddenly pictures came through of ropes and cords and net half hidden on the seabed. Then the hull of the wreck itself loomed out of the murk. As the ROV moved along the hull it came to the very sharp bow, and because the vessel was sitting so upright on the seabed, as the camera tracked down they could see the rounded forefoot of the boat. To Robert Prescott it was 'really an extremely magic moment'. But the cameras of the ROV were revealing a surprise, too. This was not a wooden Zulu class, but a steel boat of some kind. Robert Prescott was glued to the screen: 'It was a very live and active business of making hypotheses by the minute as the ROV roved to and fro. First of all we thought it might be a merchant man. It looked like the size of a small coasting trade vessel and it appeared to have cargo hatches with combings round them. Things changed quite rapidly I think when we came across a winch – a horizontal windlass type winch – which was actually lying on the seabed alongside the vessel. It perhaps became dislodged at the point of the vessel's impact with the seabed and it looked very much like a trawl winch from a fishing boat. So we think this is probably now to be identified as a steel steam trawler.'

These kinds of fishing boats were built between 1890 and 1930 in docks the length of the east coast of Britain. It could have come from Aberdeen, or Hull, or Grimsby. And some time in the first half of the twentieth century this fishing boat, with its crew of eight or nine – the youngest probably a cabin boy of around 14, the skipper perhaps a grandfather – would have set out for the North Sea fishing grounds, never to return.

'I think when you look at images like these,' says Robert Prescott 'you are really passing between two kinds of emotion. There is the excitement and the drama of what you're seeing and then there is also this element of the tragedy of all shipwrecks. One is constantly reminded of that and that never really goes away.'

On average, two Scottish fishing boats go missing every season, and it is not always clear what causes the sinking in every case. But the question remains, how did this particular fishing boat sink?

Alan Judd thinks there are five possible explanations for how a boat comes to sink in the middle of a pock mark. The first is by pure chance. Only 6 per cent of the seabed of this part of the North Sea is made up of pock marks, however, so the likelihood of a boat landing there purely by chance is small. The boat could have sunk first and then the pock mark been created by the natural action of currents. But given the size of this pock mark, the lack of strong currents and the evidence of gas escaping from the crater, it seems highly unlikely that the pock mark was caused by the boat's presence after it sank. It also seems highly unlikely that the boat foundered after its nets caught on an obstacle on the seabed. The fourth possibility is that it landed close to an existing pock mark, the sediments on the wall of the pock mark failed and it slid inside. But there is no evidence of this having happened. 'And,' says Alan, 'that leaves us with the fifth one ... the gas escape theory.'

It is not just that this seems to him the most likely explanation. Alan also considers the evidence of the Witch's Hole boat itself lends credence to this theory. For if a boat sinks – following a collision or other damage – it normally glides to the seabed and impacts heavily into the sediment. The bow or the stern is embedded in the silt. On the other hand, if it loses buoyancy because of a gas escape it falls vertically and ends up sitting on the seabed more or less upright with neither the stem nor the stern digging into the seabed.

And this is exactly the position of the Witch's Hole boat. The moment the ROV's cameras captured her on video, this was what struck the whole team watching the images.

But that is not the end of the story. For Robert Prescott adds a sixth possibility. If a boat is overwhelmed by sea – perhaps swamped by an enormous wave – then it would drop vertically, too, and end up sitting upright on the seabed. He thinks this is another likely scenario. But, as Alan Judd points out, the low barometric pressure that accompanies the kind of storm that can sink a sturdy steel steam trawler could also precipitate a release of gas. So the Witch's Hole boat could have been struggling in bad weather and then been sucked down by a gas escape. Without being able to identify the vessel and match her disappearance to the weather of the time, it is impossible to settle the argument.

There are therefore two explanations for how the boat came to sink where she did – and both seem to demand a high level of coincidence. Either she was chugging over the Witch's Hole just as a massive escape of methane gas caused the water to lose its power to hold her afloat and she was sucked to her doom; or, she was overwhelmed by gigantic waves in a bad storm and just happened to sink at the place where a big pock mark exists.

Robert Prescott admits the argument is finely balanced: 'It is extraordinary that the vessel is lying right in the centre of the Witch's Hole. That is a remarkable coincidence at the very least. And I think Alan's explanation for this is an entirely feasible one. I also think it is also quite possible that that explanation is wrong. We haven't enough evidence today to distinguish between a methane eruption that resulted in the loss of buoyancy that sank this vessel and the alternative that the vessel was overwhelmed by heavy weather, sank and happened to end up in that position. Now, Alan's point is that that is an extremely unlikely thing because of so little of the seabed being covered by pock marks and the presence of a vessel right in the centre of one of them. And he is right about that, it is an extraordinary, unlikely coincidence, but it can happen.'

And Alan is equally fair-minded: 'What is the probability of a gas escape event occurring when a ship is sailing over? Looking at it from that point of view then it is highly improbable … A betting man would not put his shirt on it … so it would be easy for scientists to say that it is not likely to happen. But improbable things do happen. Just because it is improbable, does not mean it is impossible.'

As a geologist, too, he thinks in very long time scales. The many pock marks on the bed of the North Sea were formed over 10,000 years and, though they are numerous, he says, 'The production of new events is very unlikely, so I'm still quite happy to sit on a ship in the North Sea without being worried about a gas escape event causing the ship that I'm on to founder.'

But in the year and a half since he returned from his survey of the Witch Ground, Alan Judd has received more information from other pock marks in the North Sea. Recent surveys reveal that at least two more North Sea pock marks turn out to have wrecks in them. What are the odds on that happening by coincidence? Could the North Sea in fact be Britain's very own Bermuda Triangle?

CHAPTER 7

In Search of the Real Vampires

'The vampire embodies everything that's human: good and evil, life and death.'

Michael Bell

T*hey are attractive, sophisticated and cunning; they are charming and sexy and the masters of disguise; and most important of all, they are immortal.*

The vampire is one of the most enduring and exciting creatures from the world of the supernatural. It has a history dating back 4,000 years, and in the twenty-first century it seems as popular an archetype as ever.

But more incredible even than its longevity is the fact that recent research suggests this creature has its origin not in the imagination but in concrete fact.

Driving north from Bucharest, the capital of Rumania, the road leads first across a dull agricultural plain, drained by the mighty Danube river. After one hundred kilometres or so, the road begins to rise and fall as it crosses the rolling hills of the province of Valahia. Then, as it enters the mountainous region of Transylvania, it begins to climb ever upwards. This is the land 'beyond the forests', the place popularly associated with the vampire legend, and in winter, landscape and weather conspire to convince the traveller that all the spooky stories are indeed true.

For this land of craggy mountains and deep, deep forests is both spectacular and eerie. A dripping fog hangs in the valleys so that the snow-covered peaks loom into view and disappear again mysteriously. Snow falls silently on wooden farmhouses, on bleak abandoned cemeteries, on the spires and towers and battlements of medieval castles.

As the road winds through small villages, a mixture of dour modern concrete and dark wooden buildings with steep pitched, wooden tiled roofs and wide wooden balconies, the sound of the car tyres is muffled by the snow. Farmers here still use horses and carts for farm work, and by the side of the road stand shaggy haystacks, impaled with stakes. Occasionally the still winter air is pierced by the other-worldly sound of sleigh bells and the hissing of runners as a horse-drawn sledge goes by.

This is the land made famous by Bram Stoker. For it was in Transylvania that he set his famous novel, *Dracula*. Ever since 1897 – despite the fact that surveys show most Americans, for example, do not realise it is a real place – people have flocked to Transylvania to visit the land of the vampires. Today there is a flourishing tourist trade here. In the main square of the medieval town of Bran, in the shadow of its imposing castle, stalls sell Dracula T-shirts, 'Full Moon' wine (red, of course), and pictures and statues of Dracula with lucky crucifixes. The Transylvanian Society of Dracula organises guided tours on which enthusiasts can visit places mentioned in the famous story. Tourists can buy treasures – like those owned by the fictional Count – 'at factory prices'. 'Sophisticated' newly-weds can spend their honeymoon at Castle Dracula in Borgo Pass. True aficionados can even buy 'After Life' insurance or join the Order of Transylvanian Knights.

Bram Stoker himself never came to Rumania. He was an Irish man, a man of the theatre, who knew all about melodrama and Gothic horror. Vampire stories set in Greece and Scotland, after all, were the stock-in-trade of popular Victorian theatre. But there was something different about Bram Stoker's vampire novel.

For over a century, Stoker's story has been the inspiration for hundreds of other books and films. But it was only quite recently that Raymond McNally, Professor of History at Boston College in the United States, had the idea that Bram Stoker had based his fiendish anti-hero on something more tangible than a wild imagining.

Indeed, McNally contends that Stoker did not have much of an imagination at all. He used a real context, a real place, to deepen the effect of the horror of his tale. With the precision of a railway timetable, Stoker builds up a wholly believable world where Count Dracula lives in his castle at Borgo Pass. For the first 40 pages of the novel, the reader is lulled into a false sense of security by the realism of the setting. So when things start to get strange and Count Dracula begins to reveal his supernatural side, the reader is all too ready to take the fantastical goings on as facts. Their shock is all the greater.

McNally even discovered that there had indeed been a Dracula in Transylvania, in the fifteenth century. Born in 1431, this local Prince Vlad Dracula was taken hostage by the Ottoman empire as a child. As a hostage he learnt the Turkish language and Ottoman military skills. On his return to Transylvania, where his father and brother (Radu the Handsome) appear to have both already met violent early deaths, he took up the throne of Valahia and set about driving the Ottomans from the region. A centraliser and a brutal autocrat, he quickly made enemies of the local landowners, the Saxon traders and the Church. In 1461 and again in 1462 he conducted bloody campaigns against the Ottomans.

As contemporary paintings show, the real Dracula was far from the attractive and debonair protagonist of Stoker's novel. Though considered something of a national hero by some Rumanians, McNally declares

Prince Vlad to have been 'a horror figure in his own life-time'. For he made a particular form of torture his own, earning himself the nickname Vlad the Impaler. He would impale his enemies on a stake, pinning them like butterflies to a card, letting them gradually bleed to death. And that wasn't the end of it: '... he used to dine amid his impaled victims, this Dracula, historical Dracula, and he would take bread, and dip it in the bowls of blood that were on the dinner table in front of him and then he'd slurp down the bread with the blood.'

But, although the historical Dracula – at least according to such gory stories – was a drinker of blood, he was not considered by the people of Transylvania to be a vampire. Vampires, in Rumanian legend, are something quite specific. And to make his Count a believable vampire, Bram Stoker drew on the rich traditions of eastern European folklore. Among his papers when he died were some of the sources on which he had drawn for facts about vampires. There was a copy of the academic journal *American Anthropologist*, which included a paper on the vampire tradition in North America. There was also an article by Emily Gerard, the wife of an officer in the Hungarian army, who had published a book in 1885 about the legends and superstitions of Transylvania, where her husband had for a time been posted.

In a very romantic style she wrote of how 'even in our enlightened days' the local people of the region were deeply superstitious, still believing in vampires, werewolves, fairies and ghosts. She described how, according to local tradition, the bodies of those suspected of being vampires would be exhumed and a stake driven through them. Then their opened mouths would be stuffed with garlic. Rumanian vampires, it seems, were most active at night and were terrified of the ringing of church bells, holy water and the crucifix. It was these details that Stoker incorporated into his novel. Never having visited Transylvania himself, Stoker must also have drawn some inspirational colour from Emily Gerard's descriptions of the caverns, the mountains and the forest glades – the gothic beauty of the Transylvanian countryside.

Bram Stoker's Dracula was the beginning of a massive industry. Since the turn of the twentieth century there have been more than 700 vampire movies and any number of books, cartoons, short stories and articles. Today there are websites devoted to vampires and to Dracula, and thousands of enthusiasts who both love the horror genre and, in some cases, believe themselves to be present-day vampires.

But though Bram Stoker drew on the 'real' folklore vampire tradition in part for the details of his novel, his imagination and skills as a story-teller took him much further. His vampire Count is a sophisticated and cunning individual, sexually attractive, mercurial and powerful. And it's this image of the vampire that has been taken up by the horror industry. In the movies, to become a vampire is even seen to be an attractive alternative in one way. For the vampire is immortal: he never dies.

But the vampire of tradition was a very different creature. In search of the real vampire, and the true origin of the legend, we must look beyond the stereotype of the horror film. Transylvania in the nineteenth century was not the only place where vampires were alive (or rather undead) and well (-ish) and terrorising their neighbours.

Faye Ringel is Head of the English section at the Department of Humanities at the US Coastguard Academy in New London, Connecticut. She's a cheerful, humorous woman who admits to having been interested in vampires for as long as she can remember. She devours horror stories – especially those of the cult fantasy horror writer Lovecraft – and enjoys nothing better than a no-holds-barred classic horror movie. She is also a student of the vampire in folklore, the vampire that is at the root of the vampire of the movies. She says: 'Folklore around the world has stories of revenants – that is ghosts – who are not powerless shades but rather re-animated corpses in some way ... These people who are dead are suddenly *undead* and able to interact with, and harm, the living.' She is at pains to point out that the vampire is not a ghost: 'This is a very different kind of revenant ... than the traditional ghost, who may frighten you but is not likely to kill you.'

There is no way of knowing how long this particular creature has been around. There is a Babylonian vase dating from 2500 BC that depicts a vampire. There are vampires in Greek legends. There are also stories in ancient Chinese writings of the undead who suck life from the living. In Europe, written stories about vampires start to appear in the late seventeenth century. The word first appears in English in 1734. By the late eighteenth and early nineteenth centuries there are stories in literature, newspapers and personal journals all over Europe and North America.

The vampire myth is quite precise. It is not simply a vague fear of the dead. Vampires have the power to do harm because they are the 'undead'. They are people who should be dead but for some reason aren't, and as a consequence they return to prey upon the living.

In trying to define this chilling and widely held superstition, Ray McNally points out another crucial factor and one that distinguishes the true vampire of tradition from the vampire of the movies: 'What's the key to it, is that it is always the *beloved* dead that come back. It's not the way you see it in the movies: a stranger appears in the window or something. It's someone with whom you were intimate in life … So your first reaction when you think you see them is, "Oh how great!" … If you really love someone you don't want them dead, after all …'

But it's in the fraction of a second after that first happy thought that the blood drains from the person's face and horror replaces happiness: 'The second reaction is usually: "You're supposed to be in the grave. You're dead! What are you doing walking around? And what are you going to do for sustenance? And why are you coming to see me? Are you going to lure me into communion with you?" And the only way I can go into communion with the beloved dead is to become dead myself, so with that comes the fear. It's the beloved dead (that) can lure you into the grave.'

To both Faye Ringel and Ray McNally, this fear of the dead is universal and absolutely natural, and gives a strong psychological basis to the vampire legend. As McNally points out, the dead outnumber the living to such a degree that if they rose up and returned, wishing to do us harm, we would have no chance of resisting them.

In many traditional cultures it is thought that the dead cause death and that the dead are dangerously jealous of the living. The Etruscans, for example – a vanished people who inhabited the Italian peninsula before the Romans – walled up their dead but left a little peep hole so the living could always keep an eye on them and make sure they were not moving around and causing mischief. As Faye Ringel says, 'It has to do with probably two basic human traits. One is curiosity about what lies beyond our life. And the other ... is a great fear about what lies beyond our life.'

Powerful as this explanation is, what is so fascinating about the true origin of the vampire story is that it has its roots in something far more tangible than human psychology. The real vampire can only be tracked down by examining in detail not the Hammer horror fantasy but the source of the legend, the traditional vampire of folklore. And what emerges is a very different creature from the Count Dracula of Bram Stoker's novel.

Michael Bell, a self-confessed vampire hunter, folklore specialist and author from Connecticut, describes the difference: 'If on Halloween you opened your front door and there were two figures there, a folklore vampire and a vampire from fiction, personally I would be most frightened by the folklore vampire – the disgusting corpse, which would obviously be a corpse. Whereas I think with the fictional vampire you wouldn't even recognise – unless it opened its mouth and showed its fangs – that (there) was indeed anything supernatural or something to be afraid of. What you have is an extremely attractive being that at the same time is repugnant and evil. But the evil is kept well hidden, so you don't see it on the outside. They are not disgusting on the outside. They're just dangerous.'

The vampire of Hollywood is a glamorous, seductive stranger. He (or she) wears evening dress and lives up at the castle. The vampire of folklore lives much closer to home – in your own community in fact. He, or she, is your neighbour or the crippled boy next door. Or your own wife.

Michael Bell has spent 20 years tracking down this real vampire – not in distant Transylvania, but in the American farming communities of New England at the end of the nineteenth century. It's been a fascinating journey and now he believes he has all the evidence necessary. 'How much more evidence do you need?' he asks. 'Now that you have the physical evidence, the body – to go along with the eye witnesses, the family stories, the newspaper accounts, the local histories, the diaries …?'

This journey of discovery began for Michael Bell when he caught his first glimpse of the New England vampires on Rhode Island. In the course of his regular work, he was doing a survey of the southern part of Rhode Island, talking to people and collecting family stories. In a town called Exeter a local farmer told him – a little sheepishly – that a relative of his, Mercy Brown, had been a real life vampire. Bell recalls: 'When I heard the story it seemed incredible because I really wasn't aware of this tradition. I think I'd heard about it but I didn't take it very seriously.'

From that moment on, he was hooked. He began to research Mercy's story. And it proved a surprisingly straightforward task. For this young woman had been condemned as a vampire less than 100 years before, and the story of this very modern vampire, and her slaying by her own family and friends, was told in considerable detail in the newspapers of the time.

It seems that, following the deaths of his mother and

two sisters, Edwin Brown of Essex, Rhode Island had also fallen ill. Watching him grow ever paler and more ill, his anxious father had decided to send him away to Colorado Springs in the desperate hope that the dry air would be good for his health. But not long afterwards Edwin returned to Essex. He was no better. Seeing Edwin so sick and the doctors unable to do anything for him, neighbours and friends of the family became convinced that there was something supernatural about Edwin's illness. Someone in the Brown family had become a vampire and was preying on Edwin, and if the vampire wasn't dealt with, the young man would surely die. But – according to local superstitious belief – that would not be the end of it. Once the vampire had killed Edwin, it would move on to prey on other people in the community. A delegation of neighbours came to see George Brown. They set about persuading him to exhume his dead wife and daughters to see if there were any signs that one of them was now a vampire. Or to put it more accurately, any signs that any of their bodies had been taken over by the evil spirit of a vampire.

On 17 March 1892 a macabre ritual took place in the cemetery at Essex. The corpses of 19-year-old Mercy Brown, her mother and her sister were exhumed in the presence of Edwin and George Brown. Other members of the Essex community were there at the graveside too, including the local medical examine, whose permission had been needed for the grisly plan.

Once the bodies were unearthed, it was immediately clear to the people gathered at the graveside which body was inhabited by the vampire. Mrs Brown and her elder daughter had decomposed and were now skeletons, but Mercy's body was still quite fresh. It was, after all, winter and she had only been buried two months, but this rational explanation was not the one that struck the vampire hunters. For them, the freshness of the body was a clear sign that their worst suspicions were justified. To be certain, they cut out Mercy's heart. This they found contained liquid blood. And that was their proof. They were now certain that Mercy was indeed a vampire. Convinced that this was the source of Edwin's illness, they determined to put a stop to the damage she was doing and the threat she posed to the whole community. They took her heart to a nearby stone and burnt it. The ashes they mixed with a little water. The resulting concoction was given to Edwin to drink.

It seems that the removal of the heart was enough to neutralise the vampire and so protect the community. Michael Bell interprets the making of the concoction with the ashes as a kind of folk medicine, an attempt to 'inoculate' Edwin by feeding him something of the cause of his illness. It should have saved him.

However, folk medicine was not enough. Michael Bell discovered that Edwin died a few months later, in spite of the vampire slaying in the cemetery. According to the community, though, Bell believes the process would have been considered a success, for other deaths did not follow and George Brown lived on for another thirty years, dying eventually in his eighties.

Since he first read the sad story of young Mercy Brown, Bell has followed every possible avenue to try to explain and understand the New England vampire belief. He has trawled through the newspaper archives, and turned the big pages of the local registers of births, marriages and deaths. He has scratched away the moss and lichen on gravestones in dozens of cemeteries throughout New England – some by white clapboard churches in well-kept little towns, others half over-grown and forgotten, lost in derelict countryside. He has pored over out-of-print books on local history and gathered tales and stories of the past in face-to-face interviews.

He is now certain that the belief in vampires, and the rituals considered necessary to deal with the threat they posed, was widespread in North America at least until the turn of the twentieth century. He has been able to pinpoint 20 occasions between the 1780s and the 1890s when vampires were suspected and bodies exhumed. Most were in New England but he has also found references to cases in Chicago, New York State and Ontario, Canada. The wide geographical spread and the number of references convinces him that these twenty stories are 'the tip of the iceberg ... It was a practice that was not extraordinary.'

But he soon came to realise, as he continued to track down the evidence, that to bring the New England vampires out into the light he would have to rescue the legend from the popular cliché of Count Dracula in the movies. He says: 'The Dracula image cast a shadow over the whole practice and tradition in New England to the point where people can't see it for what it really is. And it turns into a Dracula caricature, which is really unfair.'

The difference between New England vampire hunting and the vampirism of films is evident in the way the vampire hunters went about their work. To Faye Ringel, this is one of the most fascinating aspects of the historical accounts. The procedure was entirely public and open. She explains: 'This wasn't peasants with lighted torches. This wasn't people sneaking around. They seem to have done it in full daylight with everyone's knowledge.'

The digging up of Mercy Brown and the cutting up of her corpse is the latest detailed account of a vampire being dealt with in this way that Michael Bell was able to discover. It seems that by then many people – including the Medical Examiner in Mercy Brown's case who did his best to dissuade the vampire slayers and the journalists who wrote about the event for the newspapers – thought that this was a bizarre and reprehensible tradition. But earlier in the nineteenth century and before, it was clearly a tradition based on a belief that was widespread in the community.

So why did these New Englanders and the villagers of eastern Europe believe that when numbers of people in one family or one community died a vampire was at work?

As Michael Bell amassed more evidence from more vampire stories, a pattern began to emerge – a pattern of deaths that suggested to him that the root of the vampire myth was a contagious disease that would attack most members of the same family. Families like the Tillinghasts.

In this part of America, in the eighteenth and nineteenth centuries there was no real tradition of burying people only in consecrated ground. Most families had a family burial plot on their own land and that is where, with simple grave stones marking the spot, husbands and sisters, mothers and baby sons were buried.

The Tillinghast family graveyard is typical. It's only a few hundred metres from the town graveyard in Essex where Mercy was buried – and disinterred. A small collection of very simple headstones stand under trees in what is now someone's back garden.

In the last years of the eighteenth century the Tillinghast children began to fall ill. The oldest was Sarah, and in 1799 she was the first to die. Then several other children became sick, and they died too. But there was something different about the way the last six members of the family behaved while they were ill. And it was this that led to the suspicion that Sarah had become a vampire. They complained that Sarah came back to visit them at night and put pressure on their bodies.

The Tillinghast story suggested that the disease that people interpreted as an outbreak of vampirism was one that affected people at night, for this is when the vampire would visit. Victims complained that their dead relative would come at night and choke the life out of them. They would wake in the morning coughing and unable to breathe. They would also sometimes find blood on their night clothes, and as the vampire preyed on them and sucked away their life blood, so the victims would grow paler and weaker from loss of blood.

Blood then became an important theme in how survivors identified the vampire. In the days before disease was fully understood, blood was seen as the essence of life, for if you lost blood you would die. When the vampire slayers attacked the heart of the corpse, they were attacking the vampire's blood and thereby its ability to do harm. The evil was inhabiting the dead relative and the presence of blood was the proof of its power.

It was clear to Michael Bell that the vampire of the New England legend was in fact the disease tuberculosis. In many of the accounts – including the story of Edwin Brown and his sister Mercy – there was mention of the vampire's victim suffering from consumption, which was the popular name for the set of symptoms that came eventually to be identified as TB. This highly contagious disease flourishes in the kind of cramped and insanitary conditions in which people then lived. These New Englanders were mostly farmers too, and many cows in those days were infected with TB, and passed it on through their milk. TB attacks the sufferer's lungs, making it difficult to breathe, especially at night. There's even a clue in the name 'consumption' for it refers to the characteristic way the sufferers appeared to be being consumed by something. Gradually they would waste away, growing paler and thinner, and coughing blood. Eventually, most would die.

But without the body of a vampire, Michael Bell could not confirm his hunch ...

Meanwhile, on the other side of the Atlantic, another researcher was also pursuing the roots of the vampire story.

Unlike folklore expert Michael Bell, Juan Gomez Alonso is a medical man, with little previous interest in social history. He is the chief neurologist at the City Hospital in Vigo, a flourishing and lively fishing port in the north-west of Spain. In his busy hospital, Dr Gomez Alonso deals with a range of patients who suffer from diseases of the nervous system, from dementia to Parkinson's disease to migraines.

He's not a long-time vampire enthusiast, but one evening he found himself watching a vampire movie on TV. Although in his late forties, Dr Gomez Alonso had never previously seen a vampire film and he was fascinated. But it was not the charm of the fatally beautiful vampire women nor the kitsch horror clichés that caught his attention, it was the fact that before the film a documentary about vampires had stated that the vampire legend was thought to be based on a real phenomenon as yet unidentified.

Intrigued, Dr Gomez Alonso began to study the film as if he were in his clinic and the vampire was an ill patient presenting himself before the doctor. He observed the symptoms and gradually made his diagnosis.

The vampires had a horror of stimuli – of bright lights and reflecting mirrors, and strong smells like garlic. They were extremely aggressive. They showed an excessive interest in sex. All these symptoms, Dr Alonso Gomez concluded, pointed to a disease of the limbic system. This is the most primitive part of our brain – the part we share with other animals – and it is concerned with the basic appetites and emotions. Hunger, thirst, sex, anger, fear are all governed by the limbic system. The disease that best fitted these symptoms was rabies, a virus that attacks the limbic system, leading to extreme behaviour and eventually death.

As Dr Alonso Gomez watched the film he spotted more clues – the tendency of vampires to operate at night, for example. In his clinical experience, patients with 'furious' rabies often have very disturbed sleep patterns, to the extent that some completely reverse normal behaviour, and are active at night and sleep during the day. The rapacious sexual appetite of the screen vampires rang another bell with him. For he could recall stories of rabies patients becoming extremely sexually active and aggressive to the point of committing rape.

The clincher for him, though, was the way the disease is transmitted. Rabies is one of the very few diseases that is transmitted by bite – and though transmission is usually from a rabid animal, about a quarter of people with rabies will try to bite people with whom they come into contact. There is also evidence that the blood of someone who has died of rabies can stay liquid in the body after death for longer than normal – giving vampire hunters the evidence they were looking for.

Dr Gomez Alonso's diagnosis of the screen vampire is entirely new, and his is a lone voice: 'Most doctors don't think of the vampire legend as a possibility. They think it is some myth or something like that. They don't think it could have a similarity with any disease.'

Undeterred, he set out to see if he could prove his theory with historical evidence. He searched the libraries of Madrid, London, Paris and Belgrade for historical records of both rabies and vampires. And what he found was astonishing. In the late seventeenth and early eighteen centuries there were remarkable epidemics of rabies in eastern Europe. At precisely that period, accounts of vampires were also common. He found a particularly close match in the Balkans in the 1720s and 1730s. And, what seemed even more significant, at that time there were numerous accounts of vampires attacking not just people but also dogs, and in some cases killing all the dogs in a village.

Dr Gomez Alonso is convinced that he has found the true origin of the vampire legend. But experts on the folklore of vampires are not convinced. Ray McNally points out that vampires do not foam at the mouth the way people with rabies do. Michael Bell believes the connection with wolves and dogs, which carry rabies, and the biting and the aggressive behaviour suggests that the werewolf legend, which was also common in the past in eastern Europe and the Balkans, rather than the vampire legend had its origin in rabies.

But the strongest argument against the rabies hypothesis is that many of the clues taken by Dr Gomez Alonso to prove the connection are not from the original vampire of folklore. They are from the horror film vampire – with all the embellishments created during more than a century of movie clichés. The vampires who preyed on the villagers of Europe were frightened of garlic and were active at night, but they were not sexually aggressive in any way. The vampires of New England did not seem to have any aversion to strong smells or lights, nor were they thought to be sexually rapacious and though they sapped their victims' life blood they did not do it with a bite. There is no mention anywhere in the folklore in Europe or elsewhere of vampires having an exceptional bite. The famous pointed vampire fangs of the popular stereo-type are purely an invention of the silver screen.

Recently another theory has been put forward for the origin of the vampire myth, and that is the condition called porphyria. This is an inherited disorder which was only correctly identified in the twentieth century. Today porphyria is easily managed with drugs. However, in the past sufferers would have been extremely pale. Porphyria sufferers also have skin that is easily damaged by the sunlight and so in the past, before treatment was developed, they would have been forced to stay indoors in the daylight hours and only go out at night. Because of problems with their gums and nail beds, porphyria sufferers could also have developed the characteristic long nails of the vampire. They may even have appeared, as their gums retreated, to have fangs. It has been these symptoms that have led some to think that porphyria may be the origin of the vampire legend.

But others are unconvinced. Porphyria, after all, was – and is – a very rare condition. Though commoner among the royal families of Europe than among the population as a whole, sufferers were simply not present in large enough numbers across the societies of the pre-industrial world for such a universal legend to have developed around their symptoms.

Of all the folklore vampires, the ones that are best documented and so best understood are those of New England. It is in analysing these stories that there is the best hope of really understanding where the vampire story might have come from.

When the farmers and townsfolk of Connecticut and Rhode Island searched for evidence that a certain person was now a vampire they were not looking for fangs or a hearty sexual appetite. Much more important to the people who dug up Mercy Brown or the Tillinghast children were the signs they found on the dead body. They were looking for a rosy complexion, an unnaturally fat body, liquid blood at the mouth and in the heart, evidence that the coffin had been disturbed, and the sounds the corpse made, groaning or crying out in some way when a stake was driven through it.

Vampire-hunter Michael Bell, too, needed a body if he was to confirm his hunch that the origin of the vampire story – in New England at least – was the contagious disease TB.

In 1991 he got that body.

It began one afternoon when two young boys were playing on a gravel bank near a small town called Griswold in Connecticut. They were playing at sliding down the bank, and on one slide they suddenly noticed that two human skulls were rolling down the bank with them. Horrified, the boys ran straight home and told their mother. She – so the story goes – laughingly said they'd been watching too much television and refused to believe them, until the boys went back and fetched one of the skulls to show her. She rang the police, who began to investigate what they feared might be the victims of a local serial killer. Quickly, though, it became clear that these bones were old, and the State Medical Examiner contacted the local archaeology department.

Nick Bellantoni is Connecticut State Archaeologist, based at the Connecticut State Museum of Natural History at the University of Connecticut. He and his team began to excavate the area where the two skulls had been uncovered. They found a typical New England family graveyard, around 200 years old. For three months they patiently excavated the whole area and uncovered 28 graves. Most of the skeletons were conventionally arranged. They had been buried naked, their arms crossed neatly over their bodies. But then Nick uncovered another coffin, in a brick-lined grave, with the initials JB marked out on the coffin lid in nails.

When the archaeologists prised off the lid they were astonished by what they found, for the bones of JB's body had been rearranged so that what they saw lying in the coffin was a real-life skull and cross-bones. Nick Bellantoni remembers what he saw: '(JB) had been rearranged in such a way that they had taken the thigh bones or femurs from their anatomical position in the upper leg and literally crossed them right over the chest area … They had taken the skull, or cranium, from its anatomical position and completely rotated it away from facing the east.' It had been placed between the crossed thigh bones. The arms had been 'cast aside' and it was also clear that the chest cavity had been broken into, breaking some of JB's ribs.

Nick had never seen anything quite like this before.

He admits himself to have been 'befuddled' by the curious skeleton. From their archaeological work it was clear that JB had been buried in around 1820, and his grave had been broken into around five or ten years later. At first Nick guessed that it was the work of vandals who had been looking for jewels that might have been buried with the corpse. But it was clear from the other burials that these were the dead of a poor farming community, much too short of money to even bury their relatives in their clothes, let alone with anything else worth stealing. There had to be another explanation. One of the archaeological team supplied it, asking Nick if he had ever heard of the Jewitt City vampire. This town was only a couple of miles from Griswold, and the vampire was one of the stories Michael Bell had investigated. Nick Bellantoni decided to give Michael a call.

Michael remembers the call only too well – how Nick told him about the rearranged corpse and asked if he would like to come up to Griswold and take a look. He remembers his reaction, too: 'I was excited. I didn't say, "No. Too busy to come. Sorry I can't"; I said, "When would you like me to come? Tomorrow?" '

There was no written evidence of a vampire with the initials JB from that area, but everything Bell saw at the excavation convinced him that here was a man suspected of being a vampire. He could imagine the community, decimated by tuberculosis, searching for a way to stop the deaths. For some reason they had picked on JB as the possible cause of the trouble. Some years after his death they must have opened his coffin, expecting to find the tell-tale signs – the rosy, bloated body, the fresh blood still in the heart. But by then the process of decomposition had reached so far that they must only have found dry tissue and bones. Breaking through the ribs they must have searched for the heart and found nothing. Then, at a loss to know how to disable this vampire given that there was no heart or vital organs to attack, they had decided to rearrange his bones into a skull and cross-bones in a desperate attempt to control him.

For Nick Bellantoni, JB's story was particularly fascinating, for it illuminated in a concrete way the beliefs of people living in Connecticut nearly 200 years ago. Determining from the surviving evidence what people in the past ate, and what diseases they suffered from, how their homes and farms were arranged and what crops they grew are the stock-in-trade of the archaeologist. It's rare to find archaeological evidence that suggests what people believed, but that's precisely what the strange bones of JB did. Nick says, 'What we have here in the case of JB is a situation where people (were) acting on a thought world, and because of the way they acted, we can actually excavate the remains of the consequences of that belief system – and that makes it very exciting for us.'

But folklorist Michael Bell had more questions. Why did the community of Griswold pick on JB when they were looking for their vampire? And was there any evidence that he had been suffering from tuberculosis?

Nick Bellantoni completed a basic survey of the

bones from Griswold and then sent them to Paul Sledzik, Curator of Anatomical Collections, at the National Museum of Health and Medicine in Washington DC. Paul Sledzik was able to do a much more complete analysis, determining the age, height and sex of the bodies and working out from their bones what diseases they had suffered from.

Of all the bones, those of JB were the best preserved. Sledzik discovered that JB had had a disease in his left foot that had travelled up his left leg, and must have left him with a severe limp. He also discovered that JB had at some point broken his collar bone. But most interesting of all for the understanding of the vampire myth, he discovered from lesions on JB's ribs that the 'Griswold vampire' had suffered from TB.

For Bell, JB was the physical evidence he had been looking for that vampirism and TB were bound together. Not only had this man been exhumed and his limbs rearranged in a way that suggested that those who had dug him up believed him to be a vampire but the forensic analysis showed he had the disease that Bell thought was responsible for the myth in New England. It was an extremely satisfying conclusion to his long search.

But why did the people of New England pick on vampires as the explanation for TB?

Michael Bell explains: 'That connection is logical ... If you ... look at what happens to a person suffering from that disease, it's a wasting disease. That's why it's called "consumption". Your body is being consumed by some unseen and unknown force, so day after day, you become weaker and weaker, paler, and you just waste away. What's happening in fact is that your lungs are rotting and so you can't get enough oxygen to supply your body with what it needs, and you waste away.'

But it was not only these outward signs that made the consumptive look like someone who was being attacked by a vampire, it was also the symptoms of the disease itself: '… the feeling of heavy pressure on the chest, especially at night while you're sleeping, waking up coughing up blood so you might have blood on your night shirt or around the corners of your mouth … It's like something is coming at night, assaulting and draining the blood out of this person. You can see the evidence right before your eyes. It's obvious.'

So is TB at the root of the vampire story across the world? In eastern Europe as well as in North America? Michael Bell doesn't think this is necessarily so. He believes that a vampire attack could have been used to explain *any* sequence of unexplained deaths – and so any contagious disease – at a time before disease and contagion were really understood. He goes further, quoting author and student of the vampire legend, Paul Barber: 'Paul Barber's definition of a vampire is: a corpse that comes to the attention of a populace at a time of crisis and is taken as the cause of that crisis … That's a pretty broad definition, but it fits all the cases of vampirism at least in folklore history.'

In other words, the vampire was a scapegoat. The

New England vampires – like crippled JB and young Mercy Brown – were classic scapegoats. They absorbed the fear and helplessness of communities at the end of their tether as a highly contagious disease that they had no way of understanding rampaged through their midst, killing wives and fathers and children.

Nick Bellantoni paints a picture of the people who dug up JB – perhaps his own family – breaking open his ribcage and rearranging his bones into a skull and cross-bones: 'We're dealing with people who … had a great deal of fear – fear of the unknown and fear of disease and death … Most likely in this family other individuals were dying of tuberculosis, and … when all other sources of knowledge failed … they searched out alternative expla-nations. One alternative explanation is that in fact the dead are undead and capable of leaving their housing, feeding on the living and spreading the disease.'

And sometimes the behaviour of TB as it spread through a community could have encouraged the belief that it was the digging up and disabling of a vampire that had stopped the epidemic in its tracks.

Faye Ringel explains: 'Even if the epidemic did not end when the vampire was discovered and killed, you could always try again. Or you could always say, "Well the worst of it's over." And because of the strange nature of tuberculosis, especially in a small town, very often the epidemic would have indeed run its course by the time they exhumed the vampire and performed the rituals. Therefore they could really say, "Well, look!

There were no more cases after we dug up Mercy Brown, so we must have done the right thing." To this day scientists really do not know why some people are resistant to tuberculosis and others are not. In areas where there are drug-resistant strains of tuberculosis it behaves just as it did in the nineteenth century before the development of antibiotics. Everyone carries the tuberculosis bacterium. Some people develop tuberculosis. Some people never develop active tuberculosis but carry (it) ... to the end of their lives. It's all rather strange and arbitrary and even today we can't explain it. How much less could they explain in 1892?'

Faye Ringel also has a ready explanation for those who are surprised that people living in the United States a hundred years ago, literate Christian people, could have believed so utterly in the supernatural: 'Anyone who studies contemporary legends ... what we call "urban legends" knows that ... bizarre beliefs have nothing to do with level of education and everything to do with personality type ... People today who are shocked – "Well! How *can* these New Englanders possibly have believed anything so bizarre?" – themselves might believe in flying saucers or alien abductions.'

In eastern Europe there is written evidence that the community picked on all kinds of marginal people to blame as vampires when things went wrong. Someone might be thought to have become a vampire because they were illegitimate, or a hunchback or a suicide. The folklore record in New England does not suggest this was the case there.

So why did the vampire tradition die out in New England?

Bell suggests that the introduction of embalming in the United States, which became more and more popular from the 1860s, meant that corpses no longer contained blood and so the corpse no longer provided a host for the vampire. But probably much more significant was the discovery in 1882 by a German scientist that the set of symptoms known as 'consumption' that some New Englanders connected with vampires, was in fact a disease of the lungs caused by a bacterium. It was to be many years before a cure was found for TB but at least by the beginning of the twentieth century its real cause was becoming well known. A scapegoat for deaths from consumption was no longer needed.

As Faye Ringel wryly points out, 'Once tuberculosis was known to be a disease that was caused by a germ and eventually could be cured by antibiotics, then no matter how backward your family might be, they were unlikely to still believe it was caused by Aunt Mary coming back from the grave.'

The symptoms of TB account for why rural people in New England in the past believed a blood-sapping vampire was at work in their communities. But there is another explanation for why so often when the community went looking for a vampire to blame they found just what they were looking for.

William Rodriguez is Chief Forensic Anthropologist for the Armed Forces Institute of Technology in Washington DC. He examines decomposed bodies and skeletons for a living and understands the process of physical decomposition that the human body goes through. To him, it is obvious that many of the signs taken by the vampire hunters of the past to indicate a vampire's presence are simply the natural changes that take place in a body after death. In the first place, differences in body chemistry and the different physical environments produced by slightly different coffins can lead to two bodies buried at around the same time decomposing at different rates. Gas in the decomposing body may also cause the coffin to be disturbed as if the corpse had been moving. After death, as tissues shrink back, both nails and hair appear to be longer, as if they have continued to grow in the tomb. The pooling of blood in parts of the body and the increase of gas may together produce the 'rosy' and 'fat' body, well fed on blood, that relatives were looking for. Finally, when the vampire slayers drove a stake through the corpse's chest, gas escaping and travelling across the vocal chords would often have made the corpse gurgle or even appear to cry out. All these quite natural changes could have been interpreted as evidence that a vampire was present.

And Bill Rodriguez thinks that some vampire hunters may occasionally have experienced something when they exposed a dead body to the air that gave rise to another characteristic aspect of the vampire legend: '... the fact that vampires cannot become exposed to the daylight or the sun, or else they meet their death and turn to dust ... Many times you can have a body that has been placed in some type of container, such as a coffin, and has been preserved fairly well because of the very sterile type of environment. We have seen cases where ... once that is opened in the sunlight and the open air, that body will appear to decompose very rapidly, before your eyes ... within 30 minutes to hours afterwards ...'

The vampire tradition has its true origin in the way pre-scientific societies struggled to cope with diseases for which they had no explanation and against which they had no other defence, and took many of its details from the natural process of decomposition of the body. But this does not explain why Bram Stoker's *Dracula* proved so popular at the turn of the twentieth century, and is still popular at the turn of the twenty-first.

Faye Ringel sees Stoker's book as striking a real chord with its late Victorian readership:

'(*Dracula*) represents all of the fears of the turn of the twentieth century: the fear of foreigners, the fear of disease, the fear of sexuality. All of those fears can be found in *Dracula*, and also the fascination with the Gothic anti-hero – the fascination of the dangerous stranger.'

For Ray McNally the vampire will always be with us. One of its attractions is the way vampire stories are about 'thinking the unthinkable', exploring the dark areas of human experience. And, after all, evil charac-ters in literature and the other arts are far more entertaining than the good ones. He says: 'I used to think that in a scientific universe where we explain so many things this would die, this belief would go away, but it doesn't go away. It persists. And why? Because the vampire can assume a multiplicity of forms. The image changes with the changing civilisation.'

For Bram Stoker's original readers, the vampire was about the glamour of evil and about the fear of sex and foreigners. Twenty-first century vampires are more likely to be suffering from loneliness, friendless in an alienating world.

Michael Bell, too, believes that the vampire of literature and the silver screen will be with us for many years yet: 'I don't see anybody driving a stake through this beast any time soon because it embodies so many things that are attractive to people – being immortal, never dying. Although that's a curse in a way, it's still an attractive alternative to dying ... Fictional vampires aren't just ordinary people. They have superhuman strength. They're cunning. They're intelligent. They're sophisticated ... They've learned so much that they can go to a cocktail party and impress everybody with their knowledge and their sophistication and their elegance. And also they're sexy ... That's a very attractive sort of being to be ...'

FURTHER INFORMATION

Each of the incredible stories in this book has generated large numbers of books and articles, some scholarly, mostly popular. Here are some of those we found useful and/or entertaining in the making of the series.

Big Foot
Bindernagel, John A.; *North America's Great Ape: The Sasquatch*, Beachcomber Books, Canada 1998
Coleman, Loren; *The Field Guide to Bigfoot, Yeti and Other Mystery Primates Worldwide*, 1999
Krantz, Grover S.; *Big Sasquatch: Evidence*, 1999
Messner, Reinhold; *My Quest for the Yeti*, Macmillan 2000
Orchard, Vance; *Bigfoot of the Blues*, Walla Walla 1993

The Real Vampire Hunters
Barber, Paul; *Vampires, Burial and Death*, Yale 1988
Bell, Michael E.; *Food for the Dead*, Carroll & Graf, 2001
Gomez-Alonso, Juan; *Los Vampiros a la Luz de la Medicina*, Neuropress, Spain 1995
Nance, Scott; *Bloodsuckers: Vampires at the Movies*, Pioneer Books 1992

The Curse Of The Mummy
Carnarvon, The Earl of; *No Regrets*, London 1976
Cross, Stephen; *A Nile in the Sky*, (forthcoming)
Frayling, Christopher; *The Face of Tutankhamun*, Faber and Faber 1992
Reeves, Nicholas; *The Complete Tutankhamun*, Thames and Hudson 1990

The Lost City of Atlantis
Allen, J.M.; *Atlantis: The Andes Solution*, Windrush 1998
Brennan, Herbie; *The Atlantis Enigma*, Piatkus 1999
Donelly, Ignatius; *Atlantis: The Antediluvian World*, Dover 1977
Doumas, Christos; *Santorini Ekdotike*, Athenon 1995
Jordan, Paul; *The Atlantis Syndrome*, Sutton 2001
Manning, Sturt W.; *A Test of Time*, Oxbow Books, 1999

The Ten Plagues of Egypt
Baillie, Mike; *Exodus to Arthur*, Batsford 2000
Horst, Greta; 'The Plagues of Egypt' in *Zeitschrift für die alttestamentliche Wissenschaft*, Berlin 1957
Nunn, John F.; *Ancient Egyptian Medicine*, British Museum Press 1996

The Nasca Lines
Aveni, Anthony; F.; *Nasca: Eighth Wonder of the World?*, British
    Museum Press 2000
Morrison, Tony; *The Mystery of the Nasca Lines*, Nonesuch 1987
The Bermuda Triangle
Kusche, Larry; *The Bermuda Triangle Mystery Solved*, Prometheus
    1995

The Internet has transformed the quantity of material available on
many of these incredible stories. Pictures, maps, diagrams, personal
stories; the latest theories in peer reviewed journals and the oldest,
most discredited ones – all are now available online on thousands of
websites. Enter 'Atlantis', for example, into any popular search
engine, and you will get as many as 400,000 suggested sites to visit.
However, the Internet is also the favourite haunt of conspiracy theo-
rists, self-appointed experts and enthusiastic crackpots. Their works
appear with no health warning and with the same apparent
respectability as that of serious scientists online.

    This is a list of some of the web sites that are regularly updated
and that give further information on the stories covered in this book
and series.

www.island.net/~johnb/
The personal website of wildlife biologist John Bindernagel, author
of *North America's Great Ape: The Sasquatch*.

www.BFRO.net
The website of the Bigfoot Researchers Organization, "the only scientific organisation focused on the bigfoot/sasquatch mystery."

www.grahamhancock.com
The well maintained personal website of Atlantis enthusiast, writer
and broadcaster Graham Hancock. It has regular news items of
archaeological interest with particular emphasis on Atlantis. There
are links to anti-Atlantis writers as well as enthusiasts.

www.ashmol.ox.ac.uk/griffith.html
This is the information-packed website of the Griffith Institute, that
holds the Howard Carter archive. This website is still in the process
of being completed but it already has available online a fascinating
collection of Carter's excavation diaries, photographs, details of items
found in the tomb and so on.

Asterweb.jpl.nasa.gov *and* visibleearth.nasa.gov
Two amazing websites that give access to wonderful galleries of
images produced by remote sensing equipment from space. This is
the way to see Santorini island and volcano, or the longest of the
Nasca lines, as well as all kinds of other fascinating images of the
Earth – addictive.